How to do better creative work

How to d
creative

PEARSON
Prentice Hall
BUSINESS

Harlow, England • London • New York • Boston • San Francisco • Toronto
Sydney • Tokyo • Singapore • Hong Kong • Seoul • Taipei • New Delhi
Cape Town • Madrid • Mexico City • Amsterdam • Munich • Paris • Milan

o better
work

Steve Harrison

PEARSON EDUCATION LIMITED

Edinburgh Gate
Harlow CM20 2JE
Tel: +44 (0)1279 623623
Fax: +44 (0)1279 431059
Website: www.pearsoned.co.uk

First published in Great Britain in 2009

Text © Pearson Education Limited 2009

ISBN: 978-0-273-72518-3

British Library Cataloguing-in-Publication Data
A catalogue record for this book is available from the British Library

Library of Congress Cataloging-in-Publication Data
A catalog record for this book is available from the Library of Congress

10 9 8 7 6 5 4 3 2 1
13 12 11 10 09

Text design by Two Associates
Typeset in 11/14 Minion by Two Associates
Printed and bound in Great Britain by Ashford Colour Press Ltd, Gosport

The publisher's policy is to use paper manufactured from sustainable forests.

For Tommy and
Olive Harrison

Contents

Introd

uction

Does the world need another book about creative work?

Before Tim Patten, Martin Troughton and I set up shop, we asked ourselves this question: 'Does the world need another agency?' This helped concentrate our minds and led us to a positioning that proved pretty potent (and to us introducing the term 'brand response' into the marketing lexicon).

Before I wrote this book, I went through a similar exercise and asked 'Does the world need another book on creativity?' It was a lot easier to answer than the original question.

First, there aren't that many books on the 'how to' aspect of doing better creative work. Moreover, few have been written by someone who's spent the last 20 years trying, with a modicum of success, to actually do 'better creative work'.

If, during that time, you'd have asked me to explain how to go about it I'd probably have quoted the great Billy Shankly, who described football as 'a simple game made complicated by fools'.

You see, the longer I worked in the industry, the clearer and simpler things got. In fact, I became ever more convinced of the efficacy of the things you'll find described in this book: the need for not one but two big ideas, the problem/solution dynamic and the importance of relevant abruption.

But, to be honest, until recently I thought such principles were pretty obvious and there was little reason for me or anyone to sit down and write about them. Then, sometime last year, I noticed that things had changed in the industry. Which brings me to the second, more pressing reason, why I think you might find this book useful.

People I respected and admired seemed confused and unhappy. Agencies in general, and the creative fraternity in particular, appeared to be having a collective crisis of confidence.

Despondency amid the debauchery

The tipping point for me (and, I think, quite a few others) came at last year's Cannes Lions International Advertising Festival. There was some despondency amidst the debauchery. Even the Aussies looked down. Our trade magazine, *Campaign*, picked up on this and, taking the parochial view, asked 'Have the UK's creatives lost the plot?'

People in my own industry – direct marketing – certainly seemed disconcerted, especially when, on our awards night, advertising agencies threatened to steal the show. The UK contingent left in dismay and it wasn't long before *Campaign* was asking: 'Is direct marketing's golden age over?'

And the digital folk? Well, while most partied, the shrewder ones took a sober look into the future. Mark Cridge, the CEO of glue London, told me:

> 'Creatively, digital may have reached a plateau. The technical know-how that has made digital unique and unassailable to this point is becoming far more widespread. With most digital creative directors drawn from design or technology backgrounds, we have to strengthen our expertise in strong conceptual creative ideas. To get to the next level, we need the people who were weaned on *Wired* to start getting *Creative Review*. We need to grow up creatively.'

The big question was, who was going to help them reach maturity? Their advertising and direct brethren? As I looked around a strangely subdued Carlton Hotel terrace, I realised this wasn't going to happen. Because the self-belief that had once characterised the advertising and direct marketing creative fraternity had been shattered by – yes, you've guessed it – the coming of digital.

> 'To get to the next level, we need the people who were weaned on *Wired* to start getting *Creative Review*. We need to grow up creatively.'
>
> *Mark Cridge,*
> *CEO glue London*

Offline work no longer worked

In truth, it wasn't the digital creative who did the damage. It was the digital pundit, and the first blow was landed way back in 1999 by Seth Godin.

His *Permission Marketing* was an all-out attack on what he called 'interruption marketing', or all that traditional 'offline' creative work that sought to stop its prospect, engage their attention and deliver its sales message via paid-for media.

The bursting of the dotcom bubble distracted people for a while, but interest returned as online bounced back. A lot of agency folk started to believe Godin. More importantly, so did their clients. Especially when he suggested that a new era of digitally led 'permission marketing' would get them the results they wanted.

Few seem to have noticed, however, that Godin based his judgement upon a false premise. He had mistaken *bad execution* for a *broken discipline*. Essentially, what he was saying was that adverts weren't working, so therefore you'd better do away with advertising. It was a little like saying that if the NHS fails to hit government targets then the solution lies not in raising standards of detection, treatment and remedial care but in closing down all the hospitals.

It never seemed to occur to Godin that the remedy might be to do better, more effective creative work. Yet, as digital expanded, Godin's dismissal of interruption marketing became the conventional wisdom and, indeed, is now the starting point for many of today's best-selling business and marketing books.

If Godin undermined the foundations upon which competitive persuasion had been built, another book (and the numerous bestsellers, articles, conferences, seminars and blogs that it spawned) was perhaps even more damaging: Rick Levine's *The Cluetrain Manifesto*.

As with Godin, the news here was that the days of pushing a message were over.

We were entering a golden era in which technologically empowered customers pulled only those messages they wanted to receive and engaged only with those brands that they'd allow into their lives. Not only that, they would link up to share knowledge, opinions, recommendations and advice on what to buy and what to avoid. In this virtual marketplace the customer really was in control and businesses had to earn the right to join the conversation.

> Godin's dismissal of interruption marketing became the conventional wisdom and, indeed, is now the starting point for many of today's best-selling business books.

Can you spot the flaw in the pundits' argument?

This vision of Cyburbia ignored one glaring fact about modern life. The commodity all of us most lack is time. So much so that according to nVision Research, 'having time to just relax' is the UK's number-one luxury.

Of course, as books like *Groundswell* and *Wikinomics* show, there are dozens of great examples of digital communities dedicating time to this or that brand. They are, according to Malcolm Gladwell's *The Tipping Point*, the 'mavens', who are willing to talk via blogs, discussion groups, wikis, communities and forums about the object of their enthusiasm. So steeped are they in the product that they probably know more about it than both the agency folk and the marketing director. Which makes them the logical starting point for all research and development and CRM activity.

But the 'sneezers', 'alphas' and 'opinion leaders' are exceptional. The vast majority of people simply won't spend their precious time in a virtual huddle about copier printers, roadside-assist services, investment funds, pizza parlours, diesel engines, charge cards, foreign airlines, bleach or business software.

Which means a disproportionate amount of online activity is accounted for by relatively small groups. Take the blogosphere, for example. IPA-sponsored research published in January 2009 showed that of the UK's online consumers just 2.8 per cent bother to blog. Only 8.8 per cent read them and 3.7 per cent comment. As far as contributors to online chat rooms and discussion forums are concerned it is, again, a tiny fraction. Just 6.5 per cent.

It's a similar scenario with social networking sites. According to Forrester Technographics research, 25 per cent of the total number of UK internet users use social networking sites once or more a month. The remaining 75 per cent use them once a month or not at all. If you look at those who do use these sites on a daily basis, you'll see that it's overwhelmingly students and those aged 16–24. So, while some social networkers are hooked, most others are only occasional users. And, sales directors please note, given the age and occupation of the regular users, most of them are, to put it bluntly, penniless.

But what of those who do have a few bob to spend? Well, even the individual who is totally absorbed into an online community in one aspect of their lives will look to different channels in most others. For example, the new mother who cannot make a decision without consulting and sharing with Huggies Club will still enjoy the glossy, tactile pleasure of *Marie Claire* magazine when browsing for clothes, accessories and cosmetics. Like the majority of people, she'll shift between online and offline and have her purchase decisions informed by a smorgasbord of marketing communications.

How are you going to reach 'the massive passives'?

I say 'like the majority of people', but actually that's not true. Because of the people who are online there is actually a silent majority who've been totally unmoved by the *Groundswell*. According to the authors of that book, Charlene Li and Josh Bernoff, they constitute 53 per cent of Europe's digital community. These people don't even visit TripAdvisor to look at hotel reviews. Moreover they're not going to start blogging any time soon. As Faris Yacob explains in his brilliant IPA essay *I believe that children are the future*: 'The majority will continue to operate much as they ever have. Having grown up with an essentially passive relationship with media, the shift to becoming an active consumer of ideas is neither likely nor desirable.'

Make no mistake, the 'massive passives', as Yacob calls them, represent a huge market. Factor in the tens of millions who aren't even online yet, and you see how valuable these people could be.

Are your clients going to wait patiently for the 'groundswell' to eventually envelop these potential customers? And then are they going to accept a new status quo wherein the customer dictates the flow of marketing communication? What do you think? Clients will be expecting you to go out and persuade their competitors' customers to defect to them and for their own customers to spend more.

Can you do this by first getting their 'permission' with, as Seth Godin suggested, the offer of a free pen or entry to a prize draw? In some cases I'm sure this works well. But, as everyone with a letterbox knows, *Reader's Digest* have been doing this for years and such tactics tend to attract people who like prize draws and free pens – and these are not the kind of prospects you might be seeking.

Could it be achieved by getting them involved in a social networking site? Possibly, but bear in mind that even Facebook applications created by well-known brands such as MTV gather fewer than 200 users.

Can it be done by inviting these people to join you on a co-creationist, open-sourced platform? Perhaps. But as I've suggested earlier, that will work only with a minority of brand advocates, mavens and prosumers, and they will, by definition, be the hardest people to attract if they are already committed to a competitor's brand.

Or will you have to interrupt these people, both online and offline, by alerting them to the advantages they are missing … the benefit they could enjoy … the problem you could solve? In short, won't you still have to do a bit of competitive persuasion?

Getting digital messages heard above the din

I am pretty sure the answer is 'Yes'. Which is why I have written this book. And why I think that the problem/solution dynamic and relevant abruption in particular will be of interest to offline and online agencies alike. Indeed, online agencies will need to adopt these essential elements of interruption marketing as much if not more than their offline colleagues.

The sheer intensity of competition on the web leaves them no choice. As Mobbie Nazir, head of analytic development at MRM Worldwide, explained in *Campaign* magazine's 'Digital Essays':

> 'The problem is that consumers' shift towards digital media has been equalled, if not surpassed, by a shift in volume of online advertising. Add to this the now well-documented phenomenon of consumers creating and sharing their own content online and the outcome is a digital landscape that has become even more saturated with brand communications.'

Of course, the task of the online creative has been made more difficult because, as we've seen above, they've been told they have little if anything to learn from their offline peers. However, the smart ones have realised that in many cases they'll still require a big interruptive idea.

As Alix Pennycuick of Draftfcb has pointed

out in the same 'Digital Essays': 'It's the same challenge we have always faced: how to capture the public's imagination in the first place … We need to forget above-the-line and below-the-line, online or offline, and remember that, above everything else, it is the quality and creativity of the content that creates breakthrough experiences today.'

The best agencies know the answer

The best agencies buy into this. In 2008 I served as a D&AD Awards jury foreman and all the award winners in digital and direct shared one thing in common: regardless of the platform, the best work had a great interruptive idea at its heart. It was the same at *Campaign* magazine's Big Awards. In fact, it was interesting to see that the best UK digital (and indeed direct) agency on the night was that doyen of interruptive advertisers, BBH.

> All the award winners in digital and direct shared one thing in common: regardless of the platform, the best work had a great interruptive idea at its heart.

For the foreseeable future, not only will interruptive ideas continue to win the gongs, but more importantly they'll remain crucial to both the survival of brands and the generation of sales in an increasingly competitive marketplace. I'm not saying I can win you a D&AD Pencil or a Big Award, but in the following pages you'll get advice on doing work that persuades your prospect that your client's brand is more appealing and their product is better than what the competition has to offer.

As I said before, it's 'a simple game made complicated by fools'. It is also a game in which everyone plays their part.

So, there's something here for not just the creatives (in advertising, direct and digital) but also for the account handlers, the planners, the people who work in production and, last but not least, the client. Moreover, what I have to say will be just as useful to the chief executive, who wants to run a profitable, creative-led business, as the junior art director, who one day wants to be a creative leader.

It is best, and I cannot stress this enough, that everyone reads the whole thing. That way you'll all understand the roles you play and how interdependent you all are. Not only will this rounded view make you better at your job, it will also make the whole creative process more understandable – and enjoyable.

Now I'm aware that talking about making things 'enjoyable' might give the wrong impression as we all struggle through the worst economic downturn in 80 years. But, as I explain in the next chapter, doing better work isn't an indulgence. It's a driver of profitability for both client and agency alike. And it becomes even more important when things are tough.

Economic downturn? Marvellous

In hard times, clients can't afford to throw money at a marketing problem and agencies can't afford to do work that goes unnoticed. Those who never really knew what they were doing get found out – for, as the saying goes, when the tide goes out you know who has been swimming naked.

Alternatively, those who know what they're doing thrive in adversity. During the recession of 1991–3 we started to build Ogilvy & Mather Direct into the best direct marketing creative shop in the UK. Alongside likeminded agencies, we helped set in motion a creative revolution that eventually transformed the direct marketing industry worldwide (excluding North America). Likewise, we founded HTW during the downturn of 2001–3 and in those years we made a lot of money and were named both *Campaign* and *Marketing* magazines' 'Agency of the Year', largely on the strength of our creative output.

Such success is what's on offer here. So let's crack on.

What's coming up

The first chapter is aimed at pretty much everyone who wants to be more creative. It applies not just to those who are doing MPUs, press ads and mailings, but also to those who are seeking inspiration for their documents and strategies.

If Chapter 1 is aimed at the individual, then Chapter 2 is about building an environment in which everybody comes together to generate big ideas. Chapter 3 takes a closer look at big marketing ideas and explains how the best are invariably an exercise in problem/solution. Then, in Chapter 4, you'll see a detailed explanation of how to have your big marketing idea and how to express it clearly and simply.

In Chapter 5 we look at how relevant abruption can help you produce the most effective creative ideas. After that I reckon you'll have had enough theory, so in the rest of Chapter 5 and Chapter 6 there are lots of creative examples. In Chapter 5 I've chosen mainly low budget, tactical briefs, in order to show that the best work can come from the least promising beginnings. In Chapter 6 you'll see bigger strategic campaigns, which show you the old and the new ways of simultaneously building a brand and selling things.

Speaking of which, Chapter 7 is all about 'selling' and explains the five areas of knowledge you need to master in order to persuade even the most cautious client to buy your big ideas. And finally, in Chapter 8, we round everything off with a look at the most difficult job of all, that of the creative director and why it actually involves doing about five jobs at once.

OK, that's enough of the drum roll. With your permission, let's begin.

How to
be more
creative

I didn't say this earlier, but Seth Godin and his chums do have a point. A lot of what passes for interruptive work is anything but interruptive. Indeed, if you watch TV, read magazines, go online, listen to the radio or open your direct mail, you'll know that 90 per cent of marketing communications are self-indulgent, vague, dull, irrelevant wastes of the client's money, the prospect's time and the earth's resources.

I'm assuming you'd like to do work that's better. Indeed, I'm hoping you want to create work that is engaging, clear, intelligent and relevant.

As I said at the end of the introduction, this can only be achieved if everyone in the agency gets involved. So, while some chapters might be more use to an account executive and others of more interest to an art director, it is best that everyone reads everything. That way you'll understand how your actions impact on your colleagues and why the process breaks down if one of you isn't doing your bit.

This first chapter is for pretty much everyone who wants to be more creative. Whether you've 20 years' experience or you're just starting out, it's aimed at making you better at what you do. You'll see the process you should follow. You'll also discover the things you must bring to that process in order to make it work properly. But before we do all that, let's see if you're in this game for the right reasons.

Make sure you have the right attitude

You'll know if your attitude is OK by the way you answer this question: 'Why do you want to do better work?'

Perhaps it's for a portfolio full of 'edgy' and 'mould-breaking' ideas. Well, while I'm sure that might impress your mates, it's not really why you should be in this business. No, the clue lies in the last word of the last sentence: 'business'. There's a very simple reason why you should want to do better work than the competition: it will be more effective.

By that I mean it will accomplish the principal goals of all marketing communications: it will help persuade your prospect that the product you're selling is better than the competition's product, and that it is in their interest to buy it.

Make no mistake, we are in the business of competitive persuasion. And the object of your attention is the prospect who you're trying to persuade. Don't have one eye on the client. Yes, they'll be signing the invoices for the work, but they're not the ones who'll be buying the product.

Likewise, don't create for awards juries. As my first creative director, Drayton Bird, told me: 'If you try to do something that works, you might also win an award or two. But if you set out to win awards you won't have a snowball-in-hell's chance of doing something that works. And, oh yes, you'll be out of a job in six months.'

I might add that those creative teams who set out to win awards usually produce the most derivative work. That's because they're too conscious of, and influenced by, the formula that's currently in fashion. For evidence of conformity's dead hand, just look at the no-headline, no-body-copy, full-bleed-photo format that features in the press and poster categories at most awards shows.

No, if you want to be creative, don't have a copy of the Cannes Lions Annual in front of you. Clear your desk and your head and think only of the product you are selling, the proposition that sells it and the prospect you're selling it to. And always remember that, above all else, 'selling' is what you're being paid to do. In fact if, at the end of the process, you haven't helped to sell something then you haven't been creative.

This realisation came to a youthful Dave

Trott after a conversation with the great John Webster. In a recent blog, Trott recalls:

'Years back, when I was a young writer at BMP, John Webster said: "The difference between you and me is that you're a gifted amateur and I'm a professional." I asked him what that meant. He said: "At the end of the day, you'll come out of the office with something brilliant or nothing. I'll come out of the office with something brilliant or something usable." When John said that, it was like a light going on in my head, I got what he meant. This isn't art, this is business. At its best it should be a beautiful and inspiring business. But it is business.'

Get as much experience of real life as possible …

To be successful you, too, must strive to produce something that's at least 'usable' – which usually means something that will appeal to the 'man in the street'. If that man is the object of your attention, then make sure you walk the same street as him. See the world as he sees it and not through the bloodshot eyes of the denizen of the media village.

This was a point made in *Campaign* magazine by Andrew Cracknell who, after many years as a top creative director, criticised the insular attitude of that village and concluded: 'The answer clearly is to get more in touch with the real world … Maybe ad people should spend less time

As John Webster, the greatest UK adman of his generation said, 'At the end of the day, I'll come out of the office with something brilliant or something usable.'

with ad people, maybe they should listen to their partners and kids more.'

Whether 'their partners and kids' would provide the necessary reality check, I'm not sure. Maybe we'd be better off following the advice of a man who knew how to get a message across in even the most complex of multinational marketplaces. As St Paul wrote to his colleagues in the Rome office: 'Mind not high things, but condescend to men of low estate. Be not wise in your own conceits.'

I also like Philip Larkin's idea that the poet should wander 'unnoticed through life, colourless and unremarkable, wearing ordinary clothes, smoking a common brand of cigarette, hair parted to the side, queuing for the cheap seats'.

I'd recommend that you, too, queue for the cheap seats at the pictures, the theatre, galleries and exhibitions. And don't limit yourself to the type of films you always enjoy or the artists you most admire. Take yourself off into areas that make you uncomfortable. That might mean trekking across town – by public transport, of course – to listen to an avant-garde musician. Or it might mean standing in line at Leicester Square to see this summer's blockbuster movie.

Be curious about the world around you. Read a different newspaper, drink in different bars, visit a new website a day, listen to a different radio station, eat at a different type of café or restaurant and book somewhere totally different next time you're planning your holidays.

… and find out what makes people 'tick'

You'll also benefit from having a couple of proper jobs before you find a place in an agency. Don't worry about falling behind those who joined straight from college. I believe you don't really hit your stride in our business until you're through your twenties. But I suppose I would say that. I was 30 when I began as a copywriter.

While some thought it a disadvantage to be the oldest junior in the department, I consoled myself with the idea that David Ogilvy was 39 before he wrote an advertisement. More pertinently, I knew that if I studied hard enough I'd quickly get my head round doing a decent ad. My younger peers, however, would have to wait years to have their mettle tested and experience the highs, the lows and the quiet desperation in which the mass of people live their lives.

This kind of worldly attitude certainly helps you get your job in perspective. For a start, it gives you a pretty good understanding of the role that the product you're selling plays in your prospects' lives (probably very little) and the influence advertising exerts (undoubtedly even less). You also know what really is important to them and, to use an old fashioned word, what makes them 'tick'.

This was a subject that preoccupied Bill Bernbach who said: 'At the heart of every effective creative philosophy is the belief that nothing is so powerful as an insight into human nature, what compulsions drive a man, what instincts dominate his action, even though his language so often camouflages what really motivates him.'

In the mid-twentieth century, Bernbach ran Doyle Dane Bernbach, the best agency in the world. Currently that accolade goes to Crispin Porter + Bogusky. They, too, seem interested in the worldly pursuit of knowledge about people's drives and instincts. As creative partner Alex Bogusky says: 'We don't use planners. We have more anthropologists and sociologists because we really resist trendspotting.' These anthropologists and sociologists are no doubt busy finding out what makes people 'tick'. They are also helping the agency come up with bigger ideas.

Follow the process that produces big ideas

Speaking of ideas, at this point, I suppose it would help if we had a definition. The best I've heard is this: 'An idea is nothing more nor less than a new combination of old elements.' That definition comes from James Webb Young's book *A Technique for Producing Ideas*, which, while over 45 years old, is still the best primer on the subject.

Over 40 years old but still the best book on how to have a big idea.

According to Young, the process for having ideas has five stages:

1 Gather as much raw information as possible.
2 Chew it over and get your first ideas out of your system.
3 Stop thinking about the subject and let your subconscious go to work.
4 Be ready for the ideas to flow at any time.
5 Shape and develop the idea for practical usefulness.

All this might seem so self-evident you'll wonder why I bother to mention it. Yet you'd be amazed how few people really follow this process all the way through.

Let's start with stage 1. Many people trust to 'inspiration' and think they can conjure an idea out of thin air with little preparation at all. But what they'll produce will be neither original nor appropriate. You should, instead, steep yourself in your subject. The more raw information or 'old elements' you have, the more chance you have of creating a big idea. As the French scientist, Louis Pasteur, said: 'In the field of observation, chance favours only the prepared mind.'

As in science, so it is in the world of art. When Pablo Picasso created what many consider to be the greatest painting of the twentieth century, *Les Desmoiselles d'Avignon*, that act of creation owed as much to his visits to the Ethnographical Museum at Trocadéro and his discovery of African tribal carvings as it did to his tours of the Louvre and his mastery of western painting. It is not that this great artist stole. He simply searched far and wide, took that which already existed and reconfigured it into something that had never been seen before.

Give yourself enough time

An artist can spend a lifetime bringing a work to fruition. An art director, however, often has only a few days. And, panicking under the pressure of a deadline, they stop after stage 2 of Young's process. Having done the necessary home-work demanded by stage 1, they crash out their first ideas and then leave it at that.

As I suggested, often it isn't their fault. In most businesses people aren't given time to let their subconscious go to work. According to Harvard Business School's Professor Teresa Amabile, the effect is suffocating. Professor Amabile has devoted over 30 years to the analysis of creativity in business. After one exhaustive research study in 2004, she concluded that 'People were at their least creative when fighting the clock … Time pressure stifles creativity because people can't deeply engage with the problem. Creativity requires an incubation period; people need time to soak in a problem and let the ideas bubble up.'

Once the bubbling begins and, as James Webb Young says, the subconscious takes over, you need to be ready to get the ideas down on paper. So, my advice is, always have a pen handy and relish the thought of having your evenings, weekends and sleep interrupted.

There are some who feel they can stimulate the flow of ideas by going on a long walk, having a hot bath or taking in a film. Others prefer stimulants. We all know that Sherlock Holmes liked cocaine, but here's French novelist Honoré de Balzac on the effects of his drug of choice, coffee:

'Ideas quick-march into motion like battalions of a grand army to its legendary fighting ground, and the battle rages. Memories charge in, bright flags on high; the cavalry of metaphor deploys with a magnificent gallop; the artillery of logic rushes up with clattering wagons and cartridges; on imagination's orders, sharpshooters sight and fire; forms and shapes and characters rear up; the paper is spread with ink.'

I doubt if you'll get all that from a jar of Gold Blend, but you can try. And if it works, then you'll be wide awake to complete the final step of the process:

shaping and developing the idea for practical usefulness.

Unfortunately most teams neglect this. They assume that others (the account handlers, planners, flash designers, typographers, production people and their creative director) will protect their idea and bring it to fruition just as they originally saw it. They don't realise that the primary responsibility for nurturing their brainchild lies with them.

Indeed, delighted by their own ingenuity, few teams ever get the brief out again and analyse it to make sure their idea is in total alignment with the product, the prospect, the proposition and the brand. And fewer still stick with their idea through every stage of client comments and production to ensure that it is as impactful, relevant, engaging and persuasive as possible.

In short, they follow the process but they don't bring enough of themselves to it. Which brings us to the bit that really does separate John Webster's 'professionals' from his 'gifted amateurs'.

Make sure you bring four things to the process

The first two things you need are pretty intangible and I'm not really sure I can help you with them. The first is the ability to concentrate and the second is um, er, where was I …

Sorry I couldn't resist that one. The second is stamina.

As far as concentration is concerned, much of this is down to self-discipline. This is particularly important during Young's first two stages: gathering as much raw material as possible and chewing it over. Concentrating hard on a brief for the Rolls-Royce Phantom is, I'm sure you'd agree, not too difficult. Absorbing all there is to know about IBM's new Open Storage System could, however, induce attention deficit disorder in Professor Stephen Hawking.

I always found it helped if I took notes while I was going through the raw material. Few of us have the ability to retain information while we're reading. Keeping a sheet of key facts, observations, questions, ideas and apparently random thoughts will serve as a prompt. And, on good days, that sheet might even produce a headline or two as well.

On bad days, when nothing seems to be clicking, your mind will wander. When it does, you've got to go and bring it back, sit it down and get it working again. There is no other way, I'm afraid. A colleague of mine once described concentration as 'bleeding from the forehead'. He was right.

The one thing that will sustain you when everyone else has given up

All this grunt work, the processing of all the information and the final effort that

★

WRITTEN AFTER HOURS

It is after hours and most of the people have gone home.

There is a chess game in the office of the production manager and a light still burns in the cashier's cage.

From the outer room comes the untutored click of a typewriter—an office boy is taking the Y. M. C. A. course in advertising.

Across the areaway a man bends over his desk, writing. A green visor shades his eyes.

From his twenty-eighth story window as he glances up from time to time he can look down on the jewelry of lights.

It is after hours, but he works on.

He will whip his copy into finished form before he leaves.

One of the layout men has put his drawing board aside and is going out to the elevators.

Under his arm he carries a tissue pad. A new idea is stirring in his mind. It will be roughed out in pencil before morning comes.

Six months from now you will feel it tugging at your purse strings.

It is after hours and most of the people have gone home.

But out in Bronxville and Great Neck, in London and Paris, in Chicago and San Francisco—in hotel rooms, on Pullman cars, on speeding planes and ocean liners this company's people are thinking about other people's businesses, working for men who are all unaware such work is going on.

A few hurried notes scrawled on the back of an old envelope tonight may be the key to next year's most productive advertising campaign.

Between the acts at the theatre an idea may come that will make sales history.

At home beneath the reading lamp a man may solve a merchandising problem.

Once a famous trademark came back from a camping trip.

These are phases of our service that perhaps not even our own clients have ever thought of before.

There is no mention of it in our Terms and Conditions. But all our clients have been the gainer for it and will be many times again.

Why such devotion on the part of men who have already given us their day?

Of no one here is asked more than he can do. The client does not require it.

Again, why?

Anyone who deals regularly with men will tell you this is the kind of work that money alone cannot buy.

It is work done purely of free will and its real pay is pride in work well done.

Those who understand the creative mind will know just what we mean by that.

They know that the good workman, in advertising as elsewhere, asks no question save, how well can this be done?

Most of our men turned to this organization because they felt that with us they could approach their work in just that spirit.

All of us here hold that good advertising is advertising which is seen, is read and is believed—advertising which makes friends, builds good

will—advertising which returns to the advertiser his investment with a profit.

To contrive with words and pictures advertising which can do these things is a challenge to men of fine talent and quick imagination who like to write and like to draw.

It is not an easy thing to do, and if we have been unusually successful at it, that is because we love the job and have given it our best.

The men who write advertisements for the clients of this firm would succeed in any branch of journalism.

Some of them have been on university faculties. One has edited a newspaper. Others are contributors to the magazines.

They know how to appeal to the public in the printed word.

They know how to sell.

The men who lay out and design our advertising are men at the top of their profession.

They are men who, were they not advertising men, would be well known illustrators and artists.

They know how to catch the public's eye by picture and design.

They know how to sell.

The men in charge of merchandising and contact responsibilities are seasoned business men.

One of them headed a great selling organization for many years.

They know how to fit the wings of advertising to the fuselage of business.

They know how to sell.

Research department? Expert media men? Direct advertising department? Merchandising department? Export facilities?—We have them all.

We have them all developed to a degree not equaled by any other organization that we know. And these departments are all essential in the rounding out of the service this house has made its own.

But quite the finest thing we have to give to those who come to us for counsel is the high enthusiasm of our men and a devotion to their work which is measured neither by the dollar nor the clock.

This, too, was written after hours.

ERWIN, WASEY & COMPANY, INC., *Advertising*

420 Lexington Avenue, New York · 230 N. Michigan Avenue, Chicago

Here's the ad that sustained me through a lot of all-nighters and weekends spent working.

goes into 'shaping and developing the idea for practical usefulness' require the second crucial element, stamina. My first creative director, Drayton Bird, put much of my initial successes as a writer down to my 'camel-like ability to keep on going long after everyone has ****** off home'.

And it is true, I did OK because I worked harder than other people. But I was also lucky. I had fallen for the whole notion of the copywriter as a romantic ideal. Indeed, I had it pinned above my desk in the form of a house ad written over 70 years ago for a New York agency called Erwin, Wasey & Company Inc. The headline read: 'Written after hours' and beneath were 840 words of economical, evocative copy that described the solitary heroes who worked through the night to craft, hone and buff the sales messages that kept the great engine of American prosperity roaring.

I also loved the sound of the great old agencies: Batten, Barton, Durstine & Osborn … Foote, Cone & Belding … Young & Rubicam. And I was in thrall to the giants who'd stamped their names upon a century shaped by the adman's way with words and images: Ogilvy, Bernbach and Gossage. I read their books and was constantly aware of their long shadows over my keyboard. I tried to do them justice and hoped that one day I might contribute just one tiny footnote to the history they'd done so much to write.

I suggest you, too, develop your own romantic notion of what this industry is about and the part you play in it. It's the only thing that will sustain you when you find yourself up at 8.45 on a Saturday morning 'just having another look' at that brief you couldn't crack last week; taking the sixth set of client amends at 7.00 in the evening; or starting on your third layout pad at 12.30 am and knowing none of the ideas you've had so far are good enough to be presented at tomorrow's pitch.

As I've said, it's very helpful to have this romantic notion. It will certainly increase your chances of success. But be careful. I've seen a love of the industry spur individuals on to great things. I've also seen success corrupt them until the only romantic notion they have concerns their own importance. In short, if you get on, try not to become a big head.

Stay off the booze and keep active

Aside from what I've said above, I'm not sure how you summon the mix of determination and energy to stick at the task long after others have given up. I'm sure, however, that it helps if you keep yourself fit and healthy. Part and parcel of this is not drinking a lot or doing drugs. Sorry if that comes as a big disappointment to those who were hoping I was going to recommend a regime of Rimbaudesque excess. But, great poet and absinthe drinker that he was, dear old Arthur burned out at 21 and I'm sure you'll want to be picking up your Lions and Pencils until retirement age (which most of you have probably set at around 45). If so, keep your head clear and your senses alert. And if you can't abstain through the working week, make sure you never, ever drink at lunchtimes, and try to stay on the wagon on Sunday, Monday and Tuesday nights.

You should also stay active – which means making sure you're always working. If there is a pitch, volunteer your services. If there's a difficult assignment that no one can crack, tell your line manager that you'd like a go at it. If there's nothing to do, practise. Do some speculative work for existing clients and get your line manager to go and sell it. When others might be resting on their laurels, keep working on your talent.

Don't be disheartened if you don't get any immediate recognition for all this. And don't be discouraged if others seem to be getting ahead of you. In every creative industry there are always those who the muse alights upon fleetingly.

For example, there was a chap named Peter Sarstedt who, in 1967, wrote one of the greatest pop songs ever. It was called *Where do you go to, my lovely?* Perhaps you know it. He sold millions of copies and was at number one for six weeks. His eagerly awaited follow-up was called *Many coloured, semi-precious plastic Easter eggs.* After which, I'm afraid, it was more a case of *Where did you go to, Peter Sarstedt?*

Take this tip from Muhammad Ali

If you want *lasting* fame, then keep working hard. According to Malcolm Gladwell's *Outliers: The Story of Success*, to become a genius takes 10,000 concentrated hours of practice. If you'd rather just aim at being the best in your agency, then I'm sure it's considerably less. Whichever benchmark you're using, the nice thing about our industry is that a lot of your practising can be done when you're otherwise bored and kicking your heels.

For example, while you are waiting for a bus, tube or train, look around you at the ads. Think of the target audience, the product and the proposition, and then work out which of those ads will have been effective and which will have bombed. Over time this will help you develop your own creative philosophy which will, in turn, steer you subconsciously towards doing better work across all media.

An accountant, with 10 minutes to spare before the next number 11 bus, couldn't approach a stranger and ask if they needed help with their tax return. Nor could a dentist ask someone in the queue if she could have a quick look at their occlusion. But just think how lucky you are to be able to practise your craft so easily.

Yes, I suppose you could call such application hard work. But if you want to get better then that's what it takes. Listen to Muhammad Ali: 'The fight is won or lost far away from witnesses – behind the lines, in the gym and out there on the road long before I dance under those lights.' If you want to dance under those lights at the Grosvenor House or the Carlton Beach with a gong in your hand, get 'out there on the road'.

Work with people who are better than you

If you take that road then you'll discover the third and fourth elements that you need to bring to James Webb Young's process. These are the craft skills and marketing nous that come when you immerse yourself in your discipline.

Such immersion is a rite of passage in professions like the law and medicine. Yet in our industry few are encouraged to poke even a toe in the water. My advice is, get your kit off and get in there. Your agency will probably have a small training budget that isn't being used. So make it your own. Pester your boss to pay for you to go on external courses. Improve the craft skills you have and make sure you're developing new ones that complement them.

It will also help if you team up with a partner who is better than you. Why? Well, if you wanted to succeed in sport, you'd try to play with those at a slightly higher level than you because they'd pull you up to their standard. As Caroline Haxby, a Stanford Professor in Economics, has shown, this peer effect works the same with education. When you're learning your craft, you need some stiff but friendly competition to keep you moving forward.

If you progress as you'd like to then there's a chance you'll outgrow your partner and/or the agency you're working in. In that case, you should consider looking elsewhere for the challenge and stimulus that you need. If you want a really tough test, get a job at an agency that's affiliated to a network. Because the lines of briefing and approval are often more complex, it's harder to get good work out. But take it from me, as someone who spent 17 of his 20 year career at such shops, it's a lot more satisfying just because of that.

Enjoy this advantage over everyone else

In your quest for self-improvement you should also look for a mentor. If there's someone in your agency who you admire, attach yourself to them. Study what they do. Ask them how they got to be so good and then follow their example. The very good ones will probably tell you they read a few books along the way. Ask your boss to pay for those books. If you tell them you'll put them on the shelf in the agency library after you've read them, then they shouldn't object.

> Your agency will probably have a small training budget that isn't being used. So make it your own.

Not that anyone else in your agency will be too interested. It's a sad fact, but if you read just one book a year during the course of your career you'll be among the top 5 per cent most learned people in the industry. Indeed, you could probably claim guru status. Actually, let me rephrase that. It's a 'fantastic' fact. Fantastic, because it makes it so easy for you to steal an advantage over the not-so-enthusiastic amateurs who are your competitors.

I'm surprised, for example, that most people have never heard of the Volkswagen *Snowplough* commercial. But I'm amazed when I find the same ignorance of Burger King's *Subservient chicken* viral. It's like someone wanting to work in the film industry and having no clue about either *Citizen Kane* or *The Matrix*. They wouldn't tolerate this lack of knowledge on the film set, so why should it be OK in an agency?

There are, of course, people who pooh-pooh the idea of reading. Advertising chief Sir John Hegarty famously said: 'The last thing I would ever do is read a book on advertising.' Perhaps he doesn't have to. But marketing in general has suffered desperately because of this kind of philistinism.

If you don't believe me, here's an example of the industry's woeful lack of training: it is over 40 years since Stanley Pollitt and Stephen King introduced the role of the account planner, yet so great is the skills shortage and so few are the good practitioners that, two generations later,

you'd think they'd sprung their new creation upon us just two months ago.

Get your agency to pick up the tab

If you want to develop your craft skills and your marketing nous, here are the books that will help you:

- *The Book of Gossage* by Howard Luck Gossage
- *Ogilvy on Advertising* by David Ogilvy
- *Groundswell* by Charlene Li and Josh Bernoff
- *Hey Whipple, Squeeze This* by Luke Sullivan
- *Positioning* by Al Ries and Jack Trout
- *The D&AD Copy Book* edited by D&AD
- *The Tipping Point* by Malcolm Gladwell
- *A Technique for Producing Ideas* by James Webb Young
- *Truth, Lies and Advertising* by Jon Steel
- *Tested Advertising Methods* by John Caples
- *The One-to-One Future* by Don Peppers and Martha Rogers
- *Permission Marketing* by Seth Godin
- *Building Strong Brands* by David A. Aaker.

Some are out of print, but if you're determined enough you should be able to get hold of a copy. Try the industry's trade association libraries. And, of course, look on Amazon and eBay. As I said, there's a good chance you'll get your agency to pay for them even if the price is a bit steep. Also, if you're part of an agency network then a few emails hither and thither should track down the book you're looking for.

Many of these titles are classics that are often quoted but nowadays rarely read. I've recommended some that I disagree with, but who cares what I think? The important thing is that you become familiar with these books and that they help you become better at what you do.

If you're still sceptical about the importance of such learning, then let's conclude with a quote from another book you should definitely read: *More Bull*, by the industry's wisest man, Jeremy Bullmore:

'It is perfectly possible for

The wisest man in the industry recommends you read not just his book but also one or two others.

you to have a brilliant advertising idea on your first morning before lunch (I didn't). What is not possible at all is for you to know *why* it's a good idea. That's the skill that takes time to develop ... Advertising people who fail to develop a curiosity about advertising – why it exists, how it works, what it does – invariably get bored and stale and sooner or later fired.'

OK, we know that's not going to happen to you. But what we need to sort out now is whether the bosses at your agency appreciate all the effort you're making. Are they giving you the chance to shine?

If not, then leave this book on their desks open at the following page. Because the next bit is all about creating an environment in which your ideas will flourish.

How to create an environment in which better work will flourish

Do you want your agency to produce better work? All right then, I'll begin with a bit of money-saving advice and tell you what *not* to do.

Resist the temptation to hire a creative director with a great reputation in the hope that they'll transform the agency's output by sprinkling their magic dust all around their department. There is no such thing as 'magic dust'. Nor can you rely on flashes of creative brilliance to illuminate otherwise lacklustre thinking.

If there is any 'magic' to the process then it isn't performed by the creative director and their colleagues. Pretty much everybody in the agency plays their part in producing better work and the trick lies in developing an environment in which people feel free and able to make that contribution. To achieve this, all you need to do is get senior management together for an hour and ask these three questions.

> **Q1 Are we committed to creating a culture in which better work flourishes?**

The culture you're talking about has nothing to do with opera, cinema, art, literature or any of the other things that appear in TV shows that feature Melvyn Bragg or Alan Yentob and have Culture with a big C in their title. They're concerned with how Culture with a big C relates to society in general. You're only interested in how the culture you're creating affects you and your colleagues in the close-knit community that is your agency.

Most agencies that claim to have a culture actually only have a work routine into which they expect their people to fit. Yours, however, will permeate every aspect of your colleagues' working lives. It is there to help them make sense of their environment. It provides the order they need to be able to function, the structure that enables them to work out their place within the group, and the goals that provide them with a sense of individual and shared purpose.

All these come from the values you stick to, the attitudes you promote, the behaviour you encourage, the standards you uphold and the 'heroic' examples you set. From such guidelines come a sense of common interest and cohesion.

Without them, it's pretty much every man and woman for themselves. And we've all seen the horrible effect of that kind of Darwinistic chaos in the workplace. If you want to avoid it, let's move on to the next question.

Q2 What's the point of our agency?

Is it to make a healthy profit? Well, I certainly hope this is one of your aims, otherwise why are you in business? The problem is, however, that you should be able to share your number-one goal with your colleagues and your clients. And it's unlikely that you'll tempt many of your people out of bed on a cold and rainy Monday morning with the thought that 'Today's the day we all take that giant leap towards the 18 per cent year-on-year growth target our FD wrote into the Q1 forecast'.

Moreover, if your clients know that 'making the numbers' is your primary aim, they'll suspect you'll do anything to achieve it. And that, as I'm sure you'll agree, is not the basis for a good agency/client relationship.

Speaking of which, could a good agency/client relationship be your *raison d'être*? Well, obviously that makes sense, too. You're in business and they're paying the bills. But a large part of what they're paying for is your expertise and experience. And sometimes this expertise and experience will lead you to conclusions and recommendations that challenge or contradict your paymasters' assumptions

– and thus might not be met with big smiles all round at client HQ.

Moreover, if client happiness is your be all and end all, you run the risk of becoming an agency of 'yes men'. And that's not a happy place to be, either literally or figuratively.

Perhaps you think your aim should be the production of award-winning work. If so, you're wrong. No one should set out to create work with the intention of catching the eye and impressing awards judges. Your aim should be to get noticed by the prospect and for them to be so impressed by the strength of your selling idea that they buy your client's product instead of the competitions'. If you're not doing that then you shouldn't be in this business. In my view, however, this still isn't your foremost goal.

The thing that you should be striving to create and the primary focus of your efforts as managers should be this: happy and productive people.

Believe me, without happy and productive people you'll struggle to make a regular healthy profit, you'll fail to build lasting client relationships and you won't consistently produce the kind of work that you can all be proud of.

If you want more reasons for aiming for happy and productive people, try these. How expensive is it to hire and keep top quality people in your market? I suspect the answer is 'Very'. But with a workforce of happy and productive people you'll find that: (a) people don't want to leave, so you won't be looking for replacements; (b) you can pay them between 10 and 20 per cent less than market rate; (c) word gets round and you'll easily attract new recruits without having to pay the headhunters' 10–20 per cent fees; and (d) the newcomers won't even expect a rise in salary for moving from their old agency to yours – indeed you might find that some are willing to take a pay cut to work with you.

Sounds good, eh? But how do you go about producing these happy and productive people? Well, that brings me to the final question you and your senior managers need to ask yourselves.

Q3 What's our attitude towards work?

I'm afraid to say that the vast majority of people regard 'work' as a necessary evil – something they do for eight or nine hours a day in exchange for a salary that funds the 'real' (and enjoyable) part of their lives.

This selling of time by a workforce that's been reduced to interchangeable parts in the machinery of mass production is nothing new. The application of the principles of what Frederick W. Taylor termed 'scientific management' found their most famous expression in Henry Ford's Highland Park plant in Michigan. Here, the worker would take his place on the assembly line and, for upwards of 10 hours a day, bang a wing nut into a Model T, wait a few seconds, do it again, wait a few seconds, do it again, wait a few seconds … until, mercifully, it was time to go home.

Soon, alienation in the workplace had spread to the white-collar workforce. Here's the hero of Richard Yates's novel *Revolutionary Road* describing his career goals in marketing:

> 'I want some big swollen old corporation that's been bumbling along making money in its sleep for a hundred years, where they have to hire eight guys for every one job because none of them can be expected to care about whatever boring thing it is they're supposed to be doing. I want to go into that kind of place and say, "Look. You can have my body and my nice college-boy smile for so many hours a day, in exchange for so many dollars, and beyond that we'll leave each other strictly alone. Get the picture?"'

Yes the picture's depressingly clear. And familiar, too. Anyone who has read Madeleine Bunting's *Willing Slaves* or clinical psychologist Oliver James's *Affluenza* knows about the resentment many white-collar workers feel about their time at work. And this is particularly true in the UK. A study by FDS International of 13,832 workers across 23 countries showed that the UK came second only to *les misérables* of France's workforce in the league table of alienation. And that survey was conducted *before* the disintegration of the world's economy. Now the Brits' disaffection – and that of their international co-workers – is deepening by the day. As Stefan Stern summed up in the *Financial Times* in February 2009, 'Insecurity is real, not imagined. Disillusionment is widespread.'

Make everyone happy – and that includes the finance director

Anyone who has spent a few months on either the client or agency side will have shared an office with these demoralised and distracted souls. They turn up for work with no real care about who'll be receiving the communications they produce. As far as they're concerned, getting those communications out is an end in itself. They certainly get little guidance from above. Senior clients just want to spend their budgets, otherwise they'll be cut.

> If you encourage your people to strive for quality, they will be happy to work for you. They'll identify their goals with yours.

Top management in agencies need to keep the fees coming in at all costs, otherwise there'll be no chance of getting their bonuses. Meanwhile the foot soldiers look with dead eyes towards the clock and work out how many hours it is before home time. Which means the general public receives the same mass-produced marketing clichés that went out last quarter and the quarter before that and the quarter …

Is your agency like this? Of course not. Because you take the opposite attitude towards work and you know that, instead of the same old formulae and formats, everyone should be aiming to create that most rare and valuable commodity, a thing of quality.

If you encourage your people to strive for quality, they will be happy to work for you. They'll identify their goals with yours. They'll work extra hours in order to achieve those goals and they will do so not for the money you pay them but for the dignity and self-esteem they derive from their time on your premises. Unlike the unhappy wage slaves who are employed by your rivals, your staff will see little difference between their time spent in and out of work. In fact, there's even a chance they'll go home and tell their loved ones what they have achieved that day.

In short, your people will be proud of the things they produce. Better still, your clients will be proud, too. Indeed, they'll probably be willing to pay you a premium price for your work.

That'll please your finance director but, as for the rest of your people, it isn't really the money that motivates them. Let's hear again from Professor Teresa Amabile, head of the Entrepreneurial Management Unit at Harvard Business School: 'Of course, people need to feel that they're being compensated fairly. But our research shows that people put far more value on a work environment where creativity is supported, valued, and recognised. People want the opportunity to deeply engage in their work and make real progress.' She concludes that 'People are most creative when they care about their work and they're stretching their skills'.

> Everyone at the top of the company must be committed to training. If you want a creative culture to develop, you have to set the standards.

Turn everyone into a craftsman

So how do you encourage your people to care about their work?

Simple. Instil a respect for craftsmanship. Now I know this word might conjure up archaic images of the cabinet maker and the stone mason, but what I mean are the 'values' of craftsmanship.

These are as important in the digital era as they were in the Dark Ages. Richard Sennett makes this point in his book *The Craftsman*, when he writes of the computer programmer working on the Linux operating system whose rewards for contributing to its 'open source' code

are good old-fashioned pride, the respect of their peers and the refinement of technique.

The sine qua non of craftsmanship is, of course, training and this is where senior managers come back in. Everyone at the top of the company must be committed to training. If you want a creative culture to develop, you have to set the standards you want your people to attain and then teach them the necessary skills. For example, at the most fundamental level you should train them on 'How to write a brief', 'How to sell work', 'How to run a meeting' and 'How to write everything from a contact report to a strategy document'.

You'll notice I haven't mentioned creative work. That's because this fixation with 'quality' should extend to everything you do. This means every client meeting should be an enlightening experience. Each document you send should be an insightful piece of thinking. And each contact report should be a masterpiece of clarity and concision.

All these activities are creative exercises in that they require thought and deliberation prior to execution. As such, you need to give them as much focus as you would the creation of a press ad, a banner or an insert.

Get your people drunk (on learning)

Which brings me back to training. This should not be delegated to some middle-ranking 'head of training' who'll cajole their colleagues into running a session or two during everyone's lunchtime. It should be the responsibility of the individuals who run the organisation. Those at the very top should share their knowledge and show their people just how things should be done. In your agency's culture, they should set the heroic example and be the ones others aspire to be. If they are unwilling to do this, then they're neglecting their duty. And if they're incapable of leading these sessions, then we've probably identified a basic reason why the agency isn't as strong as it should be.

The leaders should also encourage the most basic form of learning: reading.

It would really help if you had a set of recommended titles (you could start with the list at the end of the last chapter). At HTW we complemented this with a Book Club whose members would pick a text and get together to discuss it over a few bottles of wine. The cost of buying the books (and wine) would, of course, be met by the agency – as also would be the fee for getting an author to come in and talk to us whenever that was possible.

While I'd recommend you focus on business titles, just getting people reading in general is now considered a great way of helping people to prick the bubble of self-hood and get insights and information from others. As the *Financial Times* recently reported, businesses as varied as Corus the steel maker, the accountancy firm BDO Stoy Hayward, Shell and Unilever are distributing books among their people. As a spokesperson for Unilever explained: '[It] is all about broadening the staff's mind and getting them to think about different concepts. When you read, you get a different perspective on things.'

Invite outside speakers in

There is, of course, a problem with getting people reading. Some don't like doing it. Especially, if you'll pardon this generalisation, youngsters. As one of the interviewees points out in *Tamara Erickson's Plugged In: The Generation Y Guide to Thriving at Work*: 'I'm not likely to read a whole book on that – a blog maybe, but not a whole book.'

If that's the case then, as well as encouraging them to overcome this childish aversion, you should provide your people with other stimuli. For example, outside speakers.

Actually let's start by identifying the 'expert' you really shouldn't get in: the consultant who'll take your people offsite and teach them such techniques as brainstorming, thought-showering, mind-mapping and lateral creative thinking.

Don't believe it when he tells you 'No idea is a bad idea'.

In my experience, this doesn't work. Some people might return from these expensive away-days starry-eyed and convinced they've hooked up with their muse. But the romance is fleeting and your business won't prosper as a result. In fact, the only person who'll make money from these gatherings is the chap who's standing in front of the Nobo board, magic marker in hand, eagerly encouraging everyone with the reassurance 'C'mon guys, no idea is a bad idea!' Believe me, that's not true. Paying his £1,500-a-day fee is a 'bad idea'.

Save your money and ask your people if, for example, there's a planner, product designer, social media expert, account director or typographer who they admire. Then offer these individuals a couple of hundred quid to come in and talk to the agency.

There are also some brilliant people in academia who would love the chance to get involved in agency life. At HTW, for example, we arranged for Alan Tapp, Professor of Marketing at Bristol Business School, to come and enrich our thinking with his occasional lectures.

> Ask your people if there's a planner, social media expert, or typographer who they admire. Then offer these individuals a couple of hundred quid to come in and talk to the agency.

And don't stop at training in the core marketing curriculum. Get an actor to advise on overcoming nerves and capturing and holding an audience's attention. Invite an RAF pilot to share their experience of decision making under pressure. See if the maître d' from the most prestigious restaurant in town will come to talk to your people about impeccable client service. Or ask a journalist to explain what it's like to write to a real deadline.

All this practical knowledge will help your people master their discipline. However, there's more to their education than this. For, to paraphrase Kipling: 'What do they know of advertising who only advertising know?'

Have crowds queuing outside your door

You can start by giving your people a monthly allowance for a trip to an event or exhibition. This might result in you signing off a lot of tickets for *The Lion King* rather than *King Lear*, but so be it. If *The Lion King* is what the public is watching, then you and your people need to sit in the upper circle, share the experience and understand its appeal.

Then, once a year, you should get the crowds queuing outside *your* doors. Have the courage of your creative convictions and put on a show of your best work from the past 12 months. This exhibition serves several purposes. It will open the eyes of clients, journalists, prospects and, yes, your own staff who may be unaware of the range of work that's being done by the agency. It'll be great for morale as it will demonstrate your confidence in your creative capabilities. And it'll strengthen your culture because it will turn a celebration of creativity into the biggest event in the agency's social calendar. Oh yes, it will be great fun, too. And fun is important.

Speaking of which, you can get your people to make exhibitions of themselves. All of them should have passions beyond the marketing world. So ask them to share those interests over a few glasses of wine in an all-agency presentation.

Better still, get them to do the presentation Pecha Kucha style. Pecha Kucha is a form of intellectual karaoke which, like the singalong variety, originated out East. It works like this: each speaker must present using 20 slides. Each of these slides is pre-programmed to be up on screen for just 20 seconds before clicking automatically to the next slide. Once the presentation is up and running, nothing can interrupt the flow. So if you're talking to the slides, then you have to time your presentation to the second.

It is terrific training for those who have to make presentations. It is also, as I said, great fun. I once organised a WPP-wide Pecha Kucha during the Cannes Lions International Advertising Festival. We

had the worldwide chief execs, executive creative directors and other panjandrums from the likes of JWT, Ogilvy, Kantor, Mindshare and Young & Rubicam, plus Sir Martin Sorrell playing to a packed Martinez Hotel. Most were great. But, despite their vast experience, some were also nervous. It'll be the same at your agency so make sure that, as Sir Martin did on that night, you lead by example.

Here's the ad that we ran in the Cannes Festival paper on the day Sir Martin Sorrell and WPP's top management presented Pecha Kucha style.

Pay them double for going on holiday

In similar vein, once a year you might also run a competition offering a month's paid leave to the person who comes up with the best project vaguely related to your agency's clients, or marketing and creativity in general. Ask everyone to write a 300-word submission. This will cause a buzz around the agency – not only during the weeks when the submissions are being written but also when the winner brings the finished project back to share with their colleagues.

And speaking of paid leave, my partner at HTW, Martin Troughton, had the remarkable idea of paying people double if they made their big holiday of the year a two-weeker instead of just seven days. (The double pay started once the second week began.) As you can imagine, it made us even more attractive to new recruits. But you might be wondering how a jaunt to, say, Buenos Aires or Sri Lanka (on double pay) could help the business?

Well, it brings us back to James Webb Young's definition of an idea as 'nothing more nor less than a new combination of old elements'. Double pay gave our colleagues the incentive to go away further and stay away longer. In so doing it helped get work out of their system and replaced it with experiences that would enrich their lives. And, as we saw in Chapter 1, the more they saw of life, the more 'old elements' they accumulated and the better their ideas became.

Of course, it's all right you forking out double pay, but as American wit and essayist Dorothy Parker said: 'You can lead a whore to culture but you can't make her think' and if your people aren't interested in learning then you're wasting your money.

Hire people who are curious – in both senses of the word

You shouldn't allow complacency in your agency. So, when hiring, avoid those who've reached a level at which they feel comfortable. The very best people are usually insecure and fear being 'found out'. This fear is the engine of self-improvement.

> You shouldn't allow complacency in your agency. So, when hiring, avoid those who've reached a level at which they feel comfortable.

And I mean the *very* best people. I once asked David Ogilvy when he finally felt secure about himself and his reputation. 'About five years ago', he replied. He was 85.

Take a leaf out of David's book yourself and also keep looking for people who are striving to be better. You'll find such individuals are interested in the industry. So, during the interview, ask the

The very best people are usually insecure and fear being 'found out'. And I mean the *very* best people. I once asked David Ogilvy when he finally felt secure about himself and his reputation. 'About five years ago', he replied. He was 85.

candidate to name the last book they read about our business. And ask them to recommend one to you. You'll also find that the best candidates are curious about the world, so ask them about their interests, where they travel and how they spend their spare time.

Which leads me to another 'curious' aspect. Some of the most talented people I've worked with have been mavericks. And even a little odd. I don't mean 'odd' in a self-conscious or mannered fashion, but in a naturally idiosyncratic way. The chances are they'll have had a couple of jobs outside the industry before they've come to you. That's even better because it means they'll already have the 'old elements' needed for quite a few big ideas. Maverick or not, when recruiting the big

question remains: 'Are they better than I was when I was at this stage in my career?' If the answer is definitely 'No', keep searching. If the answer is definitely 'Yes', hire them immediately. With your guidance, there's no telling how great they could be. All this applies not just to the creative candidates but to everyone. No matter how senior. As I said, if you're building a creative culture then it must permeate every level and affect every individual. There can be no exceptions.

The ones you should avoid

There will, I'm afraid, be those you interview who pay lip-service to the things you and your peers believe. And the more senior the vacant position, the more likely you are to find such false friends. It's not really their fault, I suppose. It's just that over the years senior people will have been influenced by the cultures of other agencies. They'll have adopted other values and ways of behaving. Having become acculturised, it will be difficult for them to abandon a belief system that might be at odds with yours. They will, of course, appear to share the values you uphold. But the sad truth is that, to many people in senior management, creativity is like fidelity: while most agree it's a good and necessary thing, when tempted by an easier option they usually succumb.

Occasionally you'll make a mistake and give someone like this a job. That's OK because, just as the white corpuscles automatically rally to reject the virus in your system, so the rest of the agency will quickly identify the foreign body in the agency. Often, they'll know before you do. Just make sure they tell you quickly.

Then, if you don't feel it's going to work out, part company as quickly as legally possible. Think of other agencies to which they'd be better suited and ring round to see if you can get them an interview. Keeping them on at your place when things aren't right would be a misery for them. It is also an unnecessary burden on those who are doing their jobs properly. Being this decisive isn't always easy. My

> To many people in senior management, creativity is like fidelity: while most agree it's a good and necessary thing, when tempted by an easier option they usually succumb.

first creative director was Chris Jones (then partner to Drayton Bird and subsequently a founder of the highly successful agency Craik Jones). He was (and I'm sure still is) an excellent art director and quite ruthless in his judgement of bad ideas. But not so in his dealings with those who produced them.

One Friday he took an art director into a room to fire him. The meeting was short. Chris apologised to the art director and said there was no easy way of doing this but there was little point in him coming in again on Monday. Miffed, the art director had a lie-in on Monday, truculently turned up for work on Tuesday and followed this new work regime for another five weeks until Chris finally and categorically gave him his cards.

How to spot a creep

That art director's presence was relatively benign. Some bad hirings are, however, poisonous. This is how they are described in the guidance notes given to those charged with selecting future officers in the British Army (you'll see that what applies to Sandhurst is also relevant in Shoreditch and Soho): 'The selection process should be particularly concerned to weed out the leader who shows impact and low brain. There are few things more dangerous than the leader who is able easily to dominate others but lacks the intellect, practicality and common sense to understand the consequences of his or her actions.'

If you're in any doubt about how to identify one of these creeps, just watch an episode of the television show *The Apprentice*. You'll see a dozen brilliant bad examples.

Once you've managed to recognise these thrusting fools and the ones who pay lip-service to your ideals, you should be OK. Indeed, with you leading by example, the culture of the agency should develop pretty quickly until it is all-encompassing.

This is very effective and very satisfying. Indeed, I can remember when someone was trying to put our agency down and they said, 'The problem with HTW is that it only exists in the minds of the people who work there'. I don't think I've ever heard a better description of an agency as a brand. This berk unwittingly paid us our greatest compliment.

Maintaining such an *esprit de corps* is crucial – and, if you follow the next bit of advice, occasionally painful.

Preserving your sense of fellowship by spilling a bit of blood …

When you're running the place you'll make decisions that are unpopular. Sometimes you'll be right and other times you'll be wrong. In either case, it's good to let your people ask you why you've done what you've done – and to tell you what they think about it. You'll get the most candid queries and comments if you let your people pop them in a box anonymously prior to quarterly question-and-answer sessions.

There are many sound and rational reasons why these meetings are a good idea. Here's one of the best. However hard you've tried to be decent, respectful and empathetic, along the way you'll have blanked, overruled or just plain pissed some people off who, because of your position, have had to swallow it. If that's the case then this is their chance to clear the air. It'll make them feel better and it might stop you being corrupted by the bit of power that you wield.

Give yourselves an hour to look through the questions (95 per cent of which will be reasonable and useful) before going out in front of the agency to try to answer them. Everyone will appreciate the openness – but, believe me, to you it will seem like a cross between participatory democracy and a public execution.

Speaking of executions, there was one time when a bit of blood letting really did wonders for our morale. We had a client who paid us well and allowed us to do good work. Unfortunately they treated our people like skivvies. Not one but two account handlers had been reduced to tears by their constant bullying.

So, one afternoon we got them in, sat them down and fired them. After that, the atmosphere in the agency was euphoric. And we could justifiably pin up Bill Bernbach's immortal words: 'A principle isn't a principle until it costs you money.'

... and avoiding a fight

Firing clients isn't great for business so, from the onset, try to get involved with only those who'll make good partners.

If you haven't got a set of criteria to guide you, how about these?

1 Can we do work that both client and agency will be proud of?
2 Will both client and agency make good money?
3 Will we all enjoy working on this account?

Number 1 should be a constant. And if you can say 'Yes' to at least one of criteria 2 and 3 then you should throw your cap in the ring. Something like this list will help when you're weighing up the pros and cons.

Inevitably you will, however, be tempted to abandon your

criteria by the prospect who'll make you loads of money but will treat your people like suppliers and gaze in mystification at the ideas you present. You may think you can take the business and protect your culture by putting the account into quarantine. But, honestly, I've never known the creation of a so-called 'village' within an agency to work. Before long the virus of expediency seeps out and infects your processes, your principles and your people.

Shifting my metaphors from the medical to the military, I'd suggest you take a tip from the Roman general, Fabius Maximus, who saved the Republic not by beating the great Carthaginian general Hannibal but by consistently avoiding the fight. He knew he had no chance of victory but, by evasive manoeuvring, kept Rome's legions, walls and honour intact.

You, too, can save your agency by refusing to become embroiled in a war of attrition against a force that might one day destroy the things you stand for. Stay out of the fight and seek those clients who know about your values and your culture and who want to enjoy the benefits that are derived from them.

As this thoughtful chap, Fabius Maximus, taught us: to survive and ultimately thrive you should pick your battles. In fact sometimes you should avoid them completely.

You'll discover who

these clients are pretty quickly during the initial chemistry sessions before a pitch begins. Find out their attitudes to producing a quality product. Listen to what they want and why they think you can help them achieve it. You'll know after the first 10 minutes whether it is going to be a happy and productive relationship.

If the chemistry is right, you should then explain how you're going to go about helping them. Which brings me, at last, to how to produce effective creative work.

Problem/ solution. Or how to have a big marketing idea

L

et's start with a warning: producing effective work is more difficult than most people think. A lot more.

First, only a handful of your prospects care about what you have to say. The vast majority is indifferent. Some people are even hostile.

Second, you're competing with hundreds of agencies for the attention of these indifferent/hostile individuals. Indeed, as every pundit seems to delight in admonishing us, we're bombarding the average consumer in the UK with upwards of 2,500 marketing communications every day. Apparently, 24 hours later, this poor soul can remember only a half a dozen of them favourably.

Which means tens of millions of pounds are wasted each day by those who fail to catch their prospects' eye. Are you ready to fight tooth and nail against the best agencies and the biggest budgets in order to make sure that it's your work that's seen and remembered? If not, you're wasting your time.

You've got an even bigger fight on your hands

And that particular fight is the easy bit, because your real battle is not with other advertisers. You're going head-to-head with every form of content and communication that vies for the attention of the reader, surfer, viewer, blogger or listener.

Like I said, most people are indifferent. No one buys their magazines for the free-standing inserts that drop out of them, even fewer log on for the overlays that invade their favourite website, and only a special kind of person goes to the front door each morning and exclaims 'Ah ha! Two pieces of unsolicited direct mail. I'll get a later train into work, pop the kettle on and have a good read.'

It's the same across all media.

Suppose, for instance, you've taken a 20 × 3 on page two of the *Daily Express*. You've spent £2,100 on the space and four weeks trying to come up with the right brief and an ad that grabs the attention and engages the reader. But are you saying anything that's more interesting than the feature that always occupies that same page and which many readers turn to automatically? Is your headline more compelling than 'Sunny periods, heavy rain later'? Not if the reader usually walks home from the railway station each evening and learns from the forecast that they should take their umbrella into work that day. The weather forecast is useful. Is your ad anything like as helpful?

And imagine you've splashed out £2,500 on a backlit billboard situated 30 feet high above a busy main road in the centre of town. Do you think the message you're beaming out from that poster is as interesting as the battered triangular tin sign on the pavement below, which tells drivers

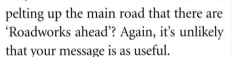
Is your message as useful as this?

pelting up the main road that there are 'Roadworks ahead'? Again, it's unlikely that your message is as useful.

Or let's say you've persuaded your client to fork out for a rich media banner campaign. Is that campaign compelling enough to compete with the Popbitch subject line announcing: 'Royal in king-size sex-scandal'? Indeed, do you think you will ever write anything that's as arresting as 'Royal in king-size sex scandal'? I doubt it.

At this point you may feel your work will never be noticed by anyone ever again. But don't give up. People who are cleverer than you and me have suffered similar despair.

Why you need not one big idea but two

The great David Ogilvy was obsessed with selling. Indeed, to make sure that everyone who worked for him shared his fixation, he printed the words 'We sell, or else' on every piece of stationery

in each of his 140 offices worldwide.

David Ogilvy had reached the reasonable conclusion that he wouldn't sell a thing if no one noticed his ads. And it was he who told us this basic truth: 'It takes a big idea to attract the attention of consumers and get them to buy your product.' He went on to warn us: 'Unless your advertising contains a big idea, it will pass like a ship in the night.' He identified the importance of the 'big idea' over 50 years ago and since then everyone, from the most callow creative course student to the most famous worldwide creative director, has made it their holy grail.

Problem is, like everyone else, they've assumed that the big *creative* idea was all they needed and that it alone will determine the success or failure of the communication.

But as the years have taught me, a big creative idea is not enough. Indeed, I believe that a big creative idea is virtually impossible unless it is preceded by a big *marketing* idea.

So what will this big marketing idea be about? Well, as we've seen, people notice things that are useful to them. So, if you're going to get their attention and impress them you need to work out how the thing you are selling can help them. To be more specific, you should look for ways in which you can solve their problems.

Find this simple problem/solution dynamic and you'll have found your big marketing idea. Once you have that, you'll be on your way to producing something truly effective. You may even make history.

If you don't believe me, just think about the work you've always admired most, and you'll find that it proceeds from a simple problem/solution marketing idea. Here's proof.

The best TV spot ever was an exercise in problem/solution ...

The greatest commercial of all time is a basic exercise in problem/solution.

What better place to start than Doyle Dane Bernbach's *Snowplough* commercial. Here, the creative task couldn't have

been more difficult. In 1960 the trend in the USA was for glamorous, gleaming automobiles that could comfortably accommodate two kids, their dog and a bowling alley in the back. It was bad enough the Volkswagen was short, ugly and squat. But its origins made it almost unsellable. As George Lois, who worked at DDB in New York during its golden age, said, 'We were advertising a Nazi car in a Jewish town'.

Worried, the agency did the sensible thing and sent the team off to West Germany to try to find their big marketing idea. While on their tour of the production line, one of them stopped to enquire as to the role of the men in the white coats. They, he was told, were the people in charge of maintaining quality control. He then asked how many of them there were. The reply astonished him. Each day there were more people checking for quality than there were cars made. But, as his smiling German host pointed out: 'That's why they are the most reliable cars in the world.'

Bingo! They'd found the solution to pretty much every car owner's problem: the design and engine faults (and the built-in obsolescence) that, in those days, consigned most cars to the scrap heap three or four years after purchase.

The VW started first time, every time. Year after year. And, as the great *Snowplough* commercial demonstrated, it started first time, every time on even the coldest, frostiest mornings. In the commercial, the VW is then seen making its way across ice sheets and upwards through a blizzard as the voice-over asks: 'Have you ever wondered how the man who drives the snowplough drives to the snowplough? This one drives a Volkswagen, so you can stop wondering.'

As the commercial ended, the snowplough roared past its driver's parked VW, and so began a campaign that ran for over 45 years. You may remember some of the wonderful commercials yourself that proceeded from that simple problem/solution dynamic, each one concluding with the wistful thought: 'If only everything in life was as reliable as a Volkswagen.'

… and that goes for the best direct mail …

Let's move on to another classic. The American Express *Quite frankly* letter. Here it's important to point out that the problem and solution is not always a practical affair like having a car that starts first time. Indeed, the problem very often exists in the mind of the prospect.

In the case of American Express there were other cards on the market that offered similar cash-free transactions. Moreover, those cards provided rolling credit, whereas Amex was a charge card that demanded repayment every 30 days. Also, the others were free, as opposed to American Express, which vetted applicants and charged an annual fee.

The big marketing idea, however, turned this last fact into the brand's advantage: anyone could carry a card that was free, but only the few would be accepted by American Express. Possession of the card became a badge of distinction. Indeed, it was the ideal status symbol in a competitive society.

With the big marketing idea already established, Bill Trembeth sat down one day at Ogilvy & Mather Direct, New York, and wrote this opening paragraph to the 1974 acquisition test mailing: 'Quite frankly, the American Express Card is not for everyone. And not everyone who applies for Cardmembership is approved.'

The next paragraph continued: 'However, because we believe you will benefit from Cardmembership, I've enclosed a special invitation for you to apply for the most honored and prestigious financial instrument available to people who travel, vacation, and entertain.'

Millions of people craved Amex's antidote for status anxiety. Which meant this most

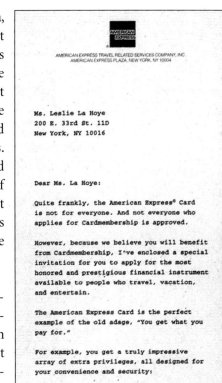

This letter did more to establish Amex as a status symbol than any ad, poster or TV campaign, and proved beyond doubt that you can build a brand in an envelope.

basic exercise in problem/solution ran as the unbeatable control from 1974 to 1986. Indeed, it could be argued that this one mailing did as much to establish Amex's exclusive positioning as any of the brand's press, poster and TV campaigns. And not just in the USA because, ultimately, *Quite frankly* was mailed around the world some 280 million times.

… and the most famous digital work, too

Next is a piece of work that didn't take 12 years to get around the world. In the digital age things happen a lot quicker. However, the same principles apply. Find the problem experienced by the prospect and show them your solution.

*Subservient chicken.*This work did for viral what *Snowplough* had done for TV commercials over 40 years earlier.

For fans of fast food the problem was lack of choice. If you wanted to get hold of your comfort food ultra quick, you couldn't expect a huge range of options. But many customers were tired of the same old same old. So Burger King's brand strategy

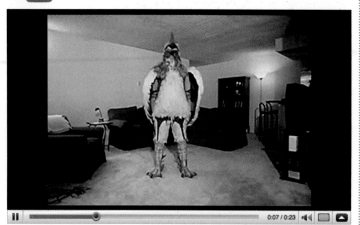

0:07 / 0:23

evolved round the solution to that problem: 'Have it your way.' When this was applied to their chicken dinners, Burger King's big marketing idea was simply adapted to become: 'Chicken any way you like it.'

And the big creative idea that dramatised that? A viral featuring a chap in a chicken suit who would perform pretty much any command you typed into your computer.

If you wanted the chicken to dance, he danced. If you wanted him to hop, he hopped. If you wanted him to … no he wouldn't do that, I'm afraid. Anyway, this was *Subservient chicken* and, as the much-respected creative director Tim Delaney said, it 'probably did more to introduce clients and agencies to the profound change that technology can make to brand communications than all the seminars and hoopla of the past few years'.

Everybody's favourites are an exercise in problem/solution, too

Perhaps the most celebrated TV spot of all time, Apple's *1984*, simply dramatised the coming of the Mac and how it would liberate the office worker from the conformist drudgery of working on a PC.

The universally acclaimed *Nike+* programme is basically the solution to the problem faced by all serious runners: theirs is a lonely calling and they crave companionship, encouragement and competition.

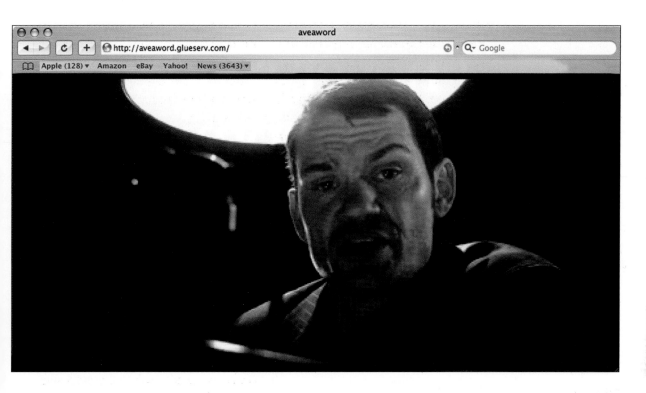

That other massive global success, the Dove *Campaign for real beauty*, is aimed purely (both literally and figuratively) at reassuring women of all ages, shapes and sizes, whose problem is their 'body image and self-esteem'.

Problem/solution lies at the core of another multi-award-winning worldwide campaign: Lynx (known as Axe in some markets). This deodorant range has little to do with stopping young men from smelling bad. It's much more fundamental than that. The problem being solved here is how to get laid.

Similarly, perhaps the best viral yet done in the UK, glue London's *'Ave a word* for the Mini Cooper S, had nothing to do with

getting the laddish audience from A to B. It was, instead, about how the car could help these young men affirm and assert their masculinity.

And what of the greatest UK poster campaign of the past 20 years? Clearly, all David Abbott and his colleagues at AMV BBDO have been offering is *The Economist*'s solution to those who are having trouble climbing the corporate ladder.

Now I may be straying here into the bit about big creative ideas – which comes in Chapter 5 – but as you'll see I've shown one of David Abbott's classics: 'I never read *The Economist*. Management Trainee, Aged 42.' I've picked this be-cause it's an excellent example of an

The Mini Cooper S had an answer to that most basic of young men's problems: how to assert their masculinity.

"I never read The Economist."

Management trainee. Aged 42.

For over 20 years *The Economist* has been offering a solution to anyone having difficulty climbing the ladder of success.

execution that dramatises the problem rather than the solution. I know a lot of clients don't like doing this. They think that such negativity reflects badly on their brand.

If your clients say something similar to you, then let them know that in the real world bad things do happen. Indeed, in the real word there are no brand guardians around to airbrush nasty occurrences from people's lives. So if their brand wants to connect with its prospects and customers, they need to get real. If they're still not convinced, give them a DVD of the UK's finest TV campaign. They'll see that for over 20 years Hamlet went to great lengths to confront the viewer with life's shitty side – and the brief moments of solace their little cigar could provide.

I've referred to some of the finest campaigns to make my point. But I'm sure that if you think about your own best work then you'll find that the problem/solution dynamic lies at its heart, too. And it will have worked in pretty much every category. I say 'in pretty much every category' but

there are two sectors where the problem/solution differs from the norm. These are charity briefs (for example Save the Children and Cancer Research UK) and social marketing briefs (for example road safety and responsible drinking).

How charity work is different …

Let's start with charity work: here the problem doesn't always affect the prospect directly. Indeed, Third World appeals by Save the Children are about as far removed from the prospect's daily experience as can be. A fund-raising appeal for Cancer Research UK might be a little closer to home, in that one in three of us will be affected by cancer in our lifetimes. However, even here the problem being described is rarely related to the prospect's immediate experience or self-interest.

And that's not the only difference from the standard brief. In the case of charities, the solution might be facilitated by the advertiser but it can only come about if the prospect gets involved. In short, it is they who provide the solution with their donations, the time they volunteer or the letters of support/protest that they're willing to write, etc.

Here's an example featuring one of the most successful charity press ads of all time. It was a humble 20 double written for Help the Aged in the late 1970s by the master of fundraising ads, Harold Sumption. The headline simply announced: 'Make a blind man see. £10.' The copy beneath explained how one simple operation could give this man his sight back – but only if the prospect was willing to stump up the ten quid that paid for that op.

The problem wasn't the prospect's, it was the old guy's. The solution wasn't Help the Aged's, it was provided by the prospect in the form of their tenner.

But what then was the ultimate benefit to the donor? What was the problem/solution as it applied to them? Well, as with all charity ads, it helped the donor feel better about themselves. They enjoyed the satisfaction that comes from solving the problems of humankind.

However, unlike many charity ads this got a lot of attention and response because everyone could imagine the problem (the misery of blindness) and most figured that, short of a miracle, the problem was irreversible. But this ad was saying that they could perform that miracle with (a) very little effort and (b) at very little cost. What an irresistible proposition.

Make a blind man see

£10

Cataracts strike thousands of elderly people in India and Africa, leaving them blinded and helpless.

Yet cataracts can be cured by a simple operation that costs as little as £10.

Help The Aged is running opthalmic programmes in India and Africa that are steadily eliminating as many cataracts as we have funds for - nearly 5000 last year. But our work cannot stop there.

Money is desperately needed to support projects that tackle the root causes of the problem - poverty, bad hygiene, malnutrition.

Please be as generous as you can, as soon as possible, because when blindness is the problem, prevention is the best cure of all.

I want to make a blind man see

To: Help The Aged, Project , FREEPOST London EC1B 1D0, Please accept my cheque/ postal order for £ _____
Name (Mr/Mrs/Miss/Ms) _____
Address _____

Postcode _____ **Help the Aged**

The problem in this classic charity ad is obviously not being experienced by the prospect.

... and why social marketing briefs are unlike any other

Social marketing briefs are similar. But there's a key difference. Here, as with most briefs, the problem again directly concerns the prospect. For example: obesity, drinking while pregnant and fire safety. So, in this respect, they are more like the standard brief.

With this social marketing campaign the solution comes when the prospect quits smoking.

Every cigarette we smoke makes fatty deposits stick in our arteries.

We'll help you give up before you clog up completely. bhf.org.uk

British Heart Foundation

As in charity work, however, the advertiser cannot solve the problem, they are only the facilitator. That solution can only happen if the prospect is so moved by the depiction of the problem that they are willing to change their behaviour. They may call on the advertiser for help and guidance but ultimately it's down to them.

Take, for example, the *Fatty cigarettes* campaign by the British Heart Foundation sponsored and in collaboration with the Department of Health. This implanted on the nation's mind the image of a cigarette oozing fat and the message that smoking clogs your arteries.

This was obviously a problem for the smoker. It was also clear that the solution could only be effected by the smoker, i.e. by them responding to the message and changing their behaviour. Thousands did just that and referral and quitting rates doubled immediately after the campaign.

If you want similar success, be mindful of the differences I've described when you're setting out to write a charity or social marketing brief. But also remember, regardless of these variations, you'll need to crack the problem/solution long before the copywriter or art director knows the job is coming their way.

If that seems like common sense, just ask yourself how often do agencies really go in search of that big marketing idea? How many understand the importance of the thinking that goes on before the creative begins? In short, how frequently do they put half-baked briefs into their creative departments in the hope that something effective might come out the other end?

'Rarely', 'Precious few' and 'Very' are, I'm afraid, the honest answers to those three questions. So, to counter such dangerous and costly practice, let's now take a look at how to deliver the big marketing idea.

We've seen how the problem/solution dynamic has worked for the biggest brands. Here's an example from a smaller business. Much smaller.

I was in Jerba in Tunisia and on my first morning set off along the beach for my constitutional. After 100 yards I saw something that really turned me off – a cracked old drainpipe spilling cloudy water out on to the beach and into the turquoise Med. Everyone was giving it a wide berth and I decided I would, too.

Three days later, however, I came that way again and to my amazement I saw, as my holiday snaps show, people splashing gaily about in the water. As I approached to investigate this cholera outbreak in the making, I saw a small wooden sign with these words etched in German: 'Thermal waters. Berber head and body massage.' Next to it sat the local chap who was obviously not only a master masseur but also a shrewd exponent of the problem/solution dynamic.

He knew his target audience – the vast majority of visitors to off-season Jerba are German senior citizens. He knew the problem that they shared: rheumatic joints and aching muscles. And he had the perfect solution: the magical balm of his (ahem) 'thermal waters'.

4.

Getting your big idea down on paper

All the agencies I worked in had strong creative reputations. I must concede, however, that this had little to do with my creative brilliance. There's a truism that more great ideas have been killed by creative directors than by anyone else. And I'm sure I administered the *coup de grâce* to a lot of potential big money-spinners and Cannes Lions winners.

Then again, our consistently good work wasn't totally down to the talent of the people whose ideas I was culling. It's true that I'd fret about falling standards when a stellar team was lured away by another agency's promise of big money. But, in most cases, we never really missed them.

No, the success wasn't down to me, the teams or anyone else in the creative department. The secret of our success lay in the standard of the briefs we received. As long as that standard was maintained through constant training and vigilance, we did better work than anyone else.

Spend twice as long on the brief as you do on the work

You should dedicate a lot of time to writing the brief. In fact, as a general rule, you should spend twice as long on the brief as you do on the creative.

If that sounds like an eternity, listen to *Campaign* magazine writing about David Patton, the client who bought the universally acclaimed *Balls* commercial for Sony BRAVIA: 'Patton says a single-minded proposition is the key to great creative work. He agrees that approving the creative idea for *Balls* took ten minutes. But, he points out, it took six months to come up with the right brief.'

I expect that Patton and his agency gave themselves a proper timing schedule. Sometimes that isn't possible. But on those kick, bollock, scramble occasions, the need for a tight brief is even more pressing. When, for example, a brief comes from the client on a Monday and creative *has*

It took them six months to get the brief right for this brilliant piece of work.

to be presented on Friday you should, if necessary, be prepared to work until Thursday afternoon in order to get the brief right. You should never, as most agencies do, put a half-finished brief into creative in the hope that the team will 'crack it'.

I must admit there were times when I stupidly allowed work into the creative department without a brief. On those occasions I'd foolishly believe the account person who had said the task was a fairly simple amend and that it was only a two-day job.

Those two-day jobs cost us dear when two weeks and two client presentations later we were still trying to get our heads round how much of the original creative had to change and how much could stay the same – and why.

Such jobs don't require the full brief that I describe below. When all that's needed is, say, an update to web content or a revision of existing copy and/or visuals, then you need only write an 'amends brief'. Just put together a one or two pager that describes clearly what needs to be changed and why. Make sure, however, that the client signs it off, as it's imperative you get their agreement on what needs to be done before work starts.

Be certain, too, that the amends don't change the existing idea. If that happens and what you need is a revised concept, then a new brief has to be written.

It pays to let the suits write the brief

Who should write the brief is a moot point. Some think it's the job of the planning dept. I reckon, however, that over-reliance on planning has led to the marginalising of account people. Or, to put it bluntly, has robbed them of the fascinating and fun aspect of their job.

A brief is a weekly workout for the marketing imagination and should ideally be written by the account people with help from: (a) the planners, who provide insight into the prospect and the problems they are experiencing; and (b) the creative team, who make their contribution during the pre-brief stage that I describe below.

This way, everyone gets involved, with the account people playing the central role in the whole process. This has several benefits. If the account people have striven to crack the big marketing idea then they'll push their creative colleagues to come up with work that really does justice to their efforts; they will also push the client harder for the requisite facts and information plus extra time if necessary; and, once the work is completed, they'll be doubly determined to sell it because they'll regard the work as their own.

Of course, it will take one or two training sessions (and ongoing help and guidance) for them to learn how to write a brief. These, however, are the most important documents your agency will produce, so it's time well invested. Here's what I would tell your trainees (both junior and senior).

What you are doing is highly creative

All you have to do is get inside the prospect's head and work out how you can help them. See the world through your prospect's eyes and try to solve their problems with your client's products or services.

It's a very creative task, because you're being asked to come up with a 'big idea'. As we've seen, big ideas don't come from a vacuum; you need to be able to draw upon a store of knowledge. This, of course, is the first stage in James Webb Young's *A Technique for Producing Ideas*.

It was also nicely summed up in this pithy poem by Sir Arthur Conan Doyle:

> *'First begin*
> *Taking in. Cargo stored*
> *All aboard, Think about*
> *Giving out. Empty ship,*
> *Useless trip.'*

To avoid useless trips, your head must be full of facts and information before you even embark on writing the brief.

You'll be relieved to know, however, that you don't have to go on this in-depth dig for detail on every single brief. Usually it's only necessary when you start on a new piece of business. After that, it's often just

a case of updating your information on the client's product or service, the competition and the customer or prospect. And then using your accumulated knowledge to write the brief that's pertinent to the task in hand.

Here's the background material you need

First and foremost, you should have a clear view of who you're selling to. This will come from the client's own research, plus any studies or information that your planning department has gathered. It certainly pays to have interviewed or attended interviews with the people you are selling to. You should also check out online forum sites to see what people really think, and use BlogPulse or Technorati to track the chatter about the brand within blogs.

After that, pick the brains of the salesforce and go and talk to call centre staff. Better still, ask if you can listen in while they're doing their job. Only after you've done all this will you be able to understand your target's point of view, get inside their minds to find out the problems they have and work out how your client's product or service can help them.

Of course, to do this you should also have 'interrogated' the product or service you're selling. You should be able to describe what it does without resorting to technical jargon. You should know when the product or service was introduced to the marketplace. You should know who the main competitors are. What your client's share of the market is in comparison to theirs. And whose product is best and why. And don't forget to ask your client. In the next chapter we'll be looking at *Grrr*, the hugely effective commercial for Honda's diesel engine. Here is Kim Papworth, the creative director of Wieden + Kennedy, the agency that produced it and a raft of other successful Honda ads, on the importance of this inside information: 'The client gives us the stuff we really need to know: for example, he'll come and relate to us exactly what an engineer at Honda has said about a particular car.'

As Wieden + Kennedy's creative director Kim Papworth knows, it pays to pick the client's brains about the things you're selling.

Dig deep now and it'll be so much easier for you later

Try to complement this kind of detail with as many case studies, testimonials, lab tests, comparative analyses, etc. as possible. Editorial comment from online and offline newspapers, and especially from trade journals and specialist customer magazines, is also extremely useful. (You should, of course, be subscribing to those trade journals and specialist magazines.) You'll find all these things provide the support to your proposition. Indeed, when you're preparing your brief, you may well find that they provide the proposition itself.

You might also find the proposition in previous advertising that has been done for the client. Very often the real reason the prospect might buy the product is buried somewhere beneath an irrelevant idea. You can't be held responsible for the bad advertising of the past, but it might lead you towards great work in the future. Showing the team previous campaigns is also important because they may never have worked on this account before and need a clear idea of how the brand is positioned and portrayed. Moreover, you'll look pretty daft presenting an idea that ran a couple of years ago.

While you're studying the old work, make sure you know the results. If one TV spot, MPU or mailpack worked better than others, then analyse why it was successful. This will guide you towards the right proposition.

It is also vital that you and the creative team know how your rivals are marketing themselves. This means much more than going on a quick trip round their website and then rooting out a couple of ads and a brochure. You should be building a portfolio of your competitors' work going back years, so you're easily able to list their claims and describe the style of their advertising.

All this background work will be a great help to you. In fact, the gathering of all the material mentioned above is designed as much for your benefit as that of the creative team. For if you know the customer intimately, the market background, your client's product and its competitors', how they compare, how they have advertised themselves previously, what the papers, the public and the pundits say about them … then your big idea will come directly from this wealth of information.

Don't worry if you don't have a USP

Now it used to be customary at this stage to set you off in search of a benefit that no one else could claim (a Unique Selling Proposition, as Rosser Reeves called it) for the product or service you were selling. And if, next time you're writing a brief, you find you have a USP then by all means consider using it. But please ensure that it is actually a benefit that the customer needs and not one dreamt up by some boffin in R&D.

It's no big deal if you don't have a USP. Very often the proposition that will work best is generic to the category.

This is explained by Patrick Barwise, Professor of Management and Marketing at London Business School, and Sean Meehan, the Martin Hilti Professor of Marketing and Change Management at

IMD, Lausanne, Switzerland, in the Marketing Society's learned journal, *Market Leader*: 'You need not offer something unique to attract business. Customers rarely buy a product because it offers something unique. Usually they buy a brand that they expect to meet their basic needs from the product category – gasoline or strategy consulting or mortgages – a bit better than or more conveniently than the competition.'

For 'meet their basic needs' read 'solve their problems'. For, as I've explained in the previous chapter, the essence of all effective advertising is problem/solution.

What I didn't say was this is: you must be sure that it is the *prospect*'s problem you are solving and not your client's. On many occasions the client will expect you to write a brief that is a direct response to *their* marketing problem. Indeed, they will expect to see *their* marketing problem described in the brief and will want a proposition that talks about that problem. If, for example, their widget sales are down 5 per cent from last quarter they may well expect to see this fact alluded to throughout the brief, and for the proposition to say something not too far removed from 'Buy our widgets, they're great'.

Try to explain to them that this will not arrest the decline in sales because there's nothing there to interest the customer.

> You must be sure that it is the *prospect*'s problem you are solving and not your client's.

The only way you'll do this is by concentrating upon the customer's problem and how your client's widgets can solve it for them. If this is then communicated by a big creative idea, then widget sales will indeed go up and the client's marketing problem will be solved.

Got that? Good. Now let's get back to writing this brief.

Never underestimate the importance of the pre-brief

OK, after you've digested all your information and used it to work out the problem/solution, you're ready to meet with the creative team for a pre-brief. This get-together is solely for your benefit. It will help you organise your thinking about the customer's problem and how your client's product or service will solve that problem.

You should also talk about your chosen media. Explain why you think it is the best route. See if they can suggest an alternative or an additional route. Also discuss if there's an opportunity to amplify the message via social media. And I don't just mean in the digital sense. Think also about the original social media: newspapers, TV and radio, and see if there's a PR angle you can exploit.

After that, describe what you think might be your proposition. Find out if they feel they can communicate such a thought. Listen to the information they feel they

will need. Do not, however, let them suggest the proposition to you. In every good team's bottom drawer there's a pile of award-winning ideas that never got sold. The less scrupulous of your creative colleagues are quite capable of retro-fitting a new proposition to suit those old ideas.

After 45 minutes you should leave them. Remember, at this juncture, you have *not* briefed the team. Your brief is *not* in the creative department. They are *not* working on your job. But now you're definitely ready to start writing your brief.

Follow these steps and you won't go wrong.

1 What is the customer problem and solution in a nutshell?

Make sure you fill this bit in first as it will focus your mind and make the rest so much easier for you. Bear in mind that if you can't fill in this section there is no point in continuing with the brief.

Write one sentence or paragraph to clearly describe the target's problem. Then in the following sentence or paragraph explain how the client's product or service will solve that problem.

(Remember what I said at the end of the last chapter about charity and social marketing briefs. There the problem might not always relate to the prospect's self-interest. That's one difference. The other is that the solution is not, as in other briefs, provided by the advertiser's product or service but by the prospect taking action and doing something themselves.)

2 What is required?

Be clear what you want the creative team to produce.

For example, please don't write, 'We need a web page'. You know as well as I do that the team will automatically assume they've more computing power and server space available than the creators of *WALL-E*. Similarly, if you just write 'We need a press ad', the team will instinctively draw the ideas up as double-page spreads. And that's not much use if all you can afford is a 20 double. It's the same with radio. No team ever willingly wrote a first script that was ever less than 60 seconds long. If all your budget allows is a 20-second spot, let the team know from the very beginning. Which brings us to:

3 What is the budget?

Be very clear about this: whether it's a TV spot or a doordrop, there is absolutely no point in putting a brief into the creative department unless the precise budget is stated.

You should also guide your team on how much they have to work with. If, for example, it *is* a doordrop, work out how much they have to spend on each item and how many will be produced. Remember £2 a doordrop for an audience of 500 doesn't get you anything like as much as £2 a doordrop for an audience of 50,000.

Finally, for the sake of clarity, show the team an example that was recently done on the same budget. Your colleagues in the production department should be able to give you a good recent example.

4 Timing plan

Be clear about exactly when you need to present work to the client. If you need a new concept then you should be allowing at least a week.

Your timing plan should include the date of the creative briefing, the work in progress and the client presentation, and be accurate right up to such hard deadlines as the air, mailing, artwork-to-newspaper date or first build, uploading, QA and/or launch dates.

5 What is the product/service you are selling?

Describe the product or service you are selling. What does it do? How does it do it? Is it special in any way? Is the way it is manufactured, designed, distributed any different? Are there any anecdotes or research relating to the product and its customers? Has anyone remarked upon its performance or capabilities? These quotes could be taken from case studies, testimonials, user forums, awards shows, blogs, lab tests, comparative analyses or editorial comment from newspapers and trade journals.

6 What is the competition doing?

Tell the team about the competition. What are their strengths and weaknesses? What has their product got going for it that your client's hasn't? Show the team how they currently advertise by giving them real examples of the competition's work.

7 How does your client currently advertise?

Give the team examples. As I said before, showing the team previous campaigns is important because they may be new to the account and need to know how the brand is positioned and portrayed, and how the product has been sold in the past.

8 What is the brand idea?

Every communication generally has two functions: (a) the tactical aim, which usually entails selling the product or service; and (b) the strategic aim of re-inforcing/refreshing the brand idea. This brand idea will be the core promise the brand makes to the consumer. It lies at the heart of the relationship that you are building with each communication and interaction you make. It will not change from brief to brief but will be constant until the agency and client agree that it needs reviewing. If the client has no brand idea then leave this section blank and ask your line manager why there is no brand idea on this piece of business.

9 Who are you talking to?

Talk about these people as individuals and write about them in the context of what you are selling. What part, if any, does the product or service play in their lives? Do they use it at the moment? Do they use the competition's alternative? If neither, how do they get by without this product or service? Are they buying the product/service for themselves? Are they using their own money? For example, in business-to-business, are they buying it on behalf of the company? If so, do they have to convince others of the product's benefits etc.?

In both business-to-business and business-to-consumer, it could be that you are writing to an 'influencer' – someone who may not even be a purchaser but who wields a lot of power in the decision-making process or the marketplace. Make sure you explain the wider role this person plays.

Likewise, describe your target in the context of the brand. Do they know the brand? If so, how do they feel about it? Are they advocates? Are they indifferent? Are they hostile? Why?

> Talk about these people as individuals and write about them in the context of what you are selling. What part, if any, does the product or service play in their lives?

10 What do they think before receiving the communication?

As I've said, briefs are an exercise in problem solving. In the very first section of the brief, you've already asked yourself: 'What problem does my prospect have that we can solve with this product or service?' Here you elaborate upon this.

Written in the first person, at the simplest level you might open up by saying 'Wouldn't it be great if …', or 'My job would be easier if …', or 'I'd be happier if …'.

If you are targeting an IT manager you might, for example, write: 'I enjoy my job, but whereas I should be concentrating on strategic planning I seem to waste most of my time maintaining the system and doing the basic repair work in the server room.'

Or for a thirtysomething woman: 'I would love to drop a couple of dress sizes by eating a low calorie diet, but that low calorie food just tastes so bland and unappetising.'

Or for a potential investor who is scared of stockmarket uncertainty: 'I know I should be taking advantage of the money markets but I'm confused by the investment market and uncertain of the products on offer.'

Or for someone who is considering buying a diesel car: 'I'd love to trade in my gas-guzzler and get a diesel but the engines are so noisy and dirty I couldn't bring myself to drive one.'

If you can describe the problem in one sentence, that's fine. If you need one or two more, then that's OK. In some instances it could be that you also want the team to be aware of other problems that the product will solve. If so, describe them here. The prospect might also have misconceptions, reservations or objections that you need the team to overcome.

> If you can describe the problem in one sentence, that's fine. If you need one or two more, then that's OK.

Likewise there may be positive opinions that you want the team to reinforce. Here is where you introduce them. But be reasonable. Make sure the medium allows for enough space or time to do justice to a longer argument.

11 What do you want them to think after receiving the communication?

This is where you describe the solution to their problem. At its simplest level you might start: 'At last I can …', or 'That's great, now I can …', or 'From now on I can …'. Try your best to make everything track. For example, the first sentence in 'What do they think before receiving the communication?' should be answered by the first sentence in 'What do you want them to think after …'.

So, for the IT manager cited above, the answer could be: 'Great, with IBM Tivoli software it's like having a fully trained IT assistant taking care of all the grunt jobs for me.'

Or for the woman who wants to lose weight: 'That's brilliant. Gordon Ramsay doesn't give his name to any old crap and his new range of ready-cooked slimmer meals should taste great.'

Or for the potential investor: 'Just what I needed: M&G will tell me the background to the market and the best products to suit my aims without any of the usual jargon.'

And for the car buyer: 'At last, Honda has come up with a diesel that doesn't make a racket and fart out fumes.'

As I said at the end of step 10 ('What do they think before receiving the communication?'), there might be other problems, misconceptions, reservations, etc. that the team needs to answer. If you've raised these in step 10, make sure you provide the team with that answer – and that everything tracks.

(As I explained at the end of Chapter 3, in charity work the problem is not being experienced by the prospect. It is being faced by the people who the charity is seeking to help. The solution is, however, provided by the prospect. In short, the whole point of charity advertising is to make the prospect so aware of and moved by the problem that they are willing to give money or time in order to make the solution happen.

Social marketing briefs differ slightly. Like all other briefs, the problem definitely is being experienced by the prospect. Here, however, the prospect is so affected by the message that their attitude and behaviour are changed to the extent that they are willing to solve the problem themselves.)

12 What do you want them to do after receiving the communication?

Never be tempted to put this in the proposition. It's a call to action and it belongs here. Keep it short and realistic: visit the website. Phone for more information. Go to the shop and buy the product. Request an update. Forward to a friend. Click here. Send a cheque. Return the coupon. That kind of thing.

13 The proposition

This is the logical conclusion of steps 10 and 11 and is the promise that's designed to stop your prospect in their tracks and get them to engage with your communication.

Please do not try to write the proposition as a headline. Others are paid to do that – your job is hard enough. Also, if you try to write it as a headline you'll be introducing your own creative idea into the process. This means that the creative team will then be trying to do *their* creative ideas about your creative idea and what results will be too far removed from the product benefit to make much sense to the prospect. So please keep your proposition simple and express it in plain language.

However do not, in the name of simplicity, be tempted to condense it into a single word. I know this approach is quite popular but it doesn't do what a good proposition is designed to do: provide guidance and direction. Here's an analogy: suppose you're on the fourth floor of a new client's offices and you're trying to find the meeting room where you are supposed to present. If you ask someone for directions and they simply say 'Downstairs' it will, while being factually correct, not give you the clear guidance you need to reach your destination. Single word propositions are likewise too vague to be much use.

For guidance on writing a good proposition, let's stay in your client's building and imagine that the presentation is over and you are waiting for a lift on the third floor. As the doors open, the personification of all your client's prospects is standing in the lift. You know the problem they face. You know the solution you have to offer. And you've got 10 seconds to express both in a single sentence before the lift reaches the ground floor. What are you going to say in those 10 seconds that will make them reply: 'I didn't know that. That's very interesting. Tell me more'?

To get this response, you must phrase your promise in terms of the customer's life and needs. This way you will write propositions that focus on a consumer benefit and you'll avoid product-focused platitudes like 'The best just gets better', 'Expect the unexpected', 'Seeing is believing' and that old bugbear of mine 'The art of [insert category]'.

If you are tempted to write something like 'The best just got better' you can turn this into a meaningful consumer promise by asking: 'What innovation, breakthrough, discovery, new widget, gizmo or gadget has been introduced that makes the best suddenly better?' Then think about the customer and ask: 'What is the problem that this will solve?'

Your proposition could be a rational fact. If you really have a single reason why you can claim a better product, you'd be mad not to use it. Remember we said that you might find this in the background research and product anecdotes. If you've done your homework, and you know who your main competitor is, then you can also do your own comparative analysis to prove your product is better, faster, cheaper, etc. It might be that someone else, editorial comment, awards juries, satisfied customers, have said it is better, faster, cheaper. Capitalise upon this.

But having discovered your product is better, please don't just trot your claim out as your proposition. Again, make sure that you focus on the customer and ask yourself: 'What is the problem that will be solved by such superiority?'

On the other hand, don't be deterred if you can't claim superiority or if the thing you're selling has no Unique Selling Proposition. As I said earlier, it might be a benefit common to every product in the category. Some of your competitors will, however, have been blind to its appeal. The others might have tried to communicate it but trotted out bland and vacuous creative that lacks either the big marketing idea or the big creative idea that you'll be striving for.

Speaking of 'the big marketing idea', whatever you do, be single-minded. When writing your proposition, do not come up with a main promise alongside a secondary thought. Avoid deft word play, constructive ambiguity and creative vagueness designed to disguise the fact you couldn't make up your mind.

Don't, for example, talk about how your product will allow the prospect to get through their work faster and enable them to present a more professional face to their customers. This is a dual proposition and each of those propositions would require a very different creative idea.

Yes I know your client might argue for both. Indeed, some clients will say 'Why stop with two? Let's shoe-horn three of four benefits in there.' That's why one of the hardest parts of writing a brief is getting the client to agree upon the single most attractive benefit and thus one thought per proposition.

> One of the hardest parts of writing a brief is getting the client to agree upon the single most attractive benefit and thus one thought per proposition.

Stand your ground. If, for example, it's a TV or radio spot, billboard, banner, MPU, SMS or viral film, then tell them it's impossible to communicate multiple benefits effectively. Quite simply, there is only room for one proposition and the argument that supports it.

If, however, you're using other media, such as a press ad, mailpack, insert, long-format infomercial, email, podcast or microsite, then explain that once you've delivered the big creative idea and its supporting argument you may be able to cover other benefits within the rest of the communication – and that those benefits will feature strongly in the support points on the brief (see step 14 below).

Insist, however, that there's one promise only in the proposition. Tell them you are trying to focus the creative team's vision so they can, in turn, focus the consumer on why they should buy the client's product.

14 The support

You know how I said the proposition should get the response 'I didn't know that. That's very interesting. Tell me more.' Well, here's the 'more'.

Write down the facts to back up your claim. And make sure they are facts – not a bit of blarney based on hearsay and wishful thinking. If you've followed my advice from the beginning then you'll have done your homework and all you'll need to do now is summarise the relevant data. It might be qualitative research, lab tests, sales figures, awards that have been won, newspaper comment, best-buy tables. Alternatively, it could be something innovative about the way the service is delivered or the product is made.

Any of this could itself be the basis of a piece of breakthrough creative. Think for a second of perhaps the most famous press ad of all time: DDB's Volkswagen *Lemon*. Mould-breaking it definitely was, but if you read the copy then you'll see how the idea proceeded from some basic factual information about the special way the cars were assembled.

> Write down the facts to back up your claim. And make sure they are facts – not a bit of blarney based on hearsay and wishful thinking.

Remember, however, that at this point you're providing information that supports the proposition – and only the proposition. Once you've done this, draw a line under those facts and write 'Other reasons why our prospect will buy this product'.

In steps 10 and 11 we spoke about the secondary problems that your product might be able to solve. Well, here's where you explain them. Please do not just write down product features; explain instead what these features mean to the consumer. How they will help them? What problems will they solve? Feel free to attach more detail in the appendices, but be sure you've read all the information and that in the brief you are clearly pointing the creative team to the relevant bits.

If you're making an offer as part of this communication, then make sure you give the details here. If it's a free guide, 20 per cent off, a free test drive, three months' free credit, two for the price of one, etc., then make sure the team know about it. They'd be mad not to make this a prominent feature of the creative. I stress, however, that this is a secondary feature. If you've decided it is not the proposition (and rarely should it be in my experience), then make sure the offer doesn't fight with the big idea.

Even if the client hasn't briefed you on an offer or an incentive, spend time thinking of how you might include one in this piece of creative. As long as it's in keeping with the brand and pertinent to the product and the proposition, then it can only increase your chances of success.

15 Tone of voice

This should come out of your understanding of the brand and the relationship the customer has with the brand. Keep it simple. Don't come up with a catch-all request for an innovative, empathetic, knowledgeable, authoritative, newsy, expert, businesslike manner.

By and large, the tone of voice should be consistent across all media. However, if you're involved in, say, an email dialogue with distinct segments then that dialogue might be conducted in an appropriately distinct fashion. For example, if you're talking with the IT professional they will converse in more technical language than the IT executive. Make sure the creative team are aware of this and give them examples of past correspondence so they know what's expected of them.

16 Mandatories/guideline

Anything that the creative team must include in the communication must be explained here, for example logos, phone numbers, web addresses, etc. Plus anything that must be avoided. I know this bit comes at the end, but please draw the team's attention to it when you're briefing them. If, for instance, you simply must include a shot from the TV commercial then make sure the team are aware of this from day one. And if, as in pharmaceuticals and financial services, the work will ultimately have to adhere to regulatory guidelines, make sure the team know the guidelines against which they'll be judged. Things like this often come to light just as you're preparing to go and present – and by then it's far too late to do anything but curse and swear.

17 Sign-off

The brief must have the signature of the senior line manager of the person who wrote it.

So, if an account director is the author then the business director must sign it off. If the account planner wrote it then it needs the input from the head of planning. After that it goes to the creative director for their approval.

Be aware that your brief may need more work after your original draft. So give yourself time by submitting the original draft to your business director/head of planning at least four days before it is supposed to go into the creative team.

When the creative director has signed it off, it should then go to the client. This is one of the most important parts of the process, yet it is also the one that's often overlooked. Indeed, very often the client is emailed the brief with no attempt by the agency to explain or discuss its content. This is madness. Getting the client to help with and buy into the brief is a crucial aspect of building good working relations. It is also a fundamental part of the selling process. We'll cover that in detail in Chapter 7. But now, let's follow the brief into the creative department.

Actually, no. Before we do that let's do a detour into your office for a second and have a quick chat about actually *writing* the brief.

A few, mainly short, words on how to actually write a brief – and pretty much anything else

What I'm about to say won't just help when you're writing briefs. It will also improve your documents, emails, letters, speeches, etc. And, if you write copy for advertising, digital or direct it will make you better at your job.

Whatever you're writing, there's one thing that will always be the same. What you're doing can be daunting. And some people, when faced by a blank screen, adopt an awkward writing style that's far removed from their natural tone of voice.

The easy way to find your natural tone is to imagine you are sitting opposite the person you're writing to and that you're talking to them. Then write as you speak. Be conversational. (If you're writing copy, remember you are communicating on behalf of the brand, so take your steer from 'Tone of voice' – step 15 above – and write as the brand would speak.)

If you tend to talk in business buzz words and marketing clichés, try not to – they betray the fact that you don't really know what you're talking about. If you can't stop, then at least keep them out of your writing. By using these pre-packaged phrases you are avoiding thinking about what it is that you really want to say. Instead of using language properly, it is using you.

If your audience speaks a jargon that's peculiar to their industry or sector then be careful. If you use that jargon then you run the risk of making a mistake and damaging your credibility. Moreover, when you're writing a brief you should avoid the jargon completely. Remember your audience here are your creative colleagues and they probably won't understand such peculiar terminology.

Use four-letter words

Which words will they understand? Well, of the 80 most used words in the English language, 78 have an Anglo-Saxon root. These are the short, simple words you use in everyday speech. 'Make' not 'manufacture'. 'Know' not 'acquaint'. 'Many' not 'myriad'. 'Move along' not 'expedite'. 'Meet' not 'rendezvous' and certainly not 'interface'. 'Free' not 'complimentary'. 'Eat' not 'consume'. 'About' not 'approximately'. 'Get' not 'acquire'. 'Start' not 'initiate'. 'Take part' not 'participate'. 'Think' not 'conceptualise' or, that laughable gift from our American friends, 'ideate'. Everyone is cognisant of, sorry, knows these words, and if you use them you'll help the reader along. If you don't believe me

> The easy way to find your natural tone is to imagine you are sitting opposite the person you're writing to and that you're talking to them. Then write as you speak.

when I say familiarity makes for easy reading, try this test.

Speed-read while you count the number of letter Fs:

**FABULOUS FACES ARE OFTEN THE PRODUCT
OF A LIFETIME OF
GOOD LIVING COMPLEMENTED BY
THE BENEFITS OF NATURE**

How many? Three? Four? There are, in fact, seven. During a quick read your eyes and brain are processing the longer, less common words and tend to ignore the details of the shorter, more familiar words (like the three 'of's.) Which means when you use short and familiar words the brain spends less time deciphering the form of the words and more time absorbing their meaning.

Briefs aside, there is one short word you should use in everything you write. 'You' should appear three times more than 'I' or 'we'. This will help you write about the subject from the viewpoint of the reader.

It will also help you with the most difficult bit – getting started. Your first paragraph of copy or your first paragraph in a document should reflect where the reader's opinion, experience, knowledge or attitude is at that moment. With that as your starting point you should, like any good salesman, use empathy to deftly move them on to where you want them to be.

How to earn $40,000 per job

Perhaps the finest copywriter/salesman of all time was Bill Jayme, who earned $40,000 for each mailpack he wrote in the USA in the 1980s. Bill was in no doubt about the secret of his success. 'I have an unusual gift for empathy' he told the *The New York Times* magazine in 1990. In all his mailings, the starting point was always the space inside the head of the prospect. For example, in one classic letter for *Pyschology Today* he asked: 'Do you close the bathroom door even when you're the only one home?'

You, too, will go far by seeing the world through the eyes of others. And not just at work. For instance, if you've a hot date this Saturday, try using 'you' three times more than 'I' throughout the evening. I assure you that your date will think you're the most interesting person and the finest conversationalist they've met in years. And they'll probably still be thinking that as you're waving them off

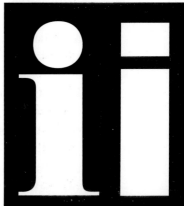

Follow the lead of David, this book's designer. He has made the book easier for you to read by choosing a serif face instead of a sans serif face. He has also set the columns at around forty characters per line, which makes it easier for your eye to go back and forth. Likewise he has avoided using CAPITAL LETTERS LIKE THIS because he knows they are difficult to comprehend. And he has otherwise avoided reversing light type out of a dark background because, as you can see, it is hard to read.

after breakfast on Sunday morning.

Back at work you should also use short sentences. The average length of a sentence in this book is 9.81 words. Which is one of the reasons you've got this far.

You should use short paragraphs as well. Try to have just one thought per paragraph.

And make sure each of them tracks one after another in a logical sequence.

People are more likely to read your copy if you break it up with subheads

Use these subheads to précis the content and to give the reader an overall sense of what's in it for them. Most people will initially scan your work to see if it's worth reading. Used properly, those subheads will make them decide in your favour.

You won't achieve all of the above in your first draft. In fact, first drafts are to your finished piece what a rough scamp is to the ad that finally appears in a magazine. So set your work aside and then come back to it with fresh eyes. Writers in all disciplines know that achieving something good takes time. And the best writers are fiercely critical of their own work. Here, for example is Stephen Sondheim cringing at his words to *I feel pretty* from his musical *West Side Story*.

> Writers in all disciplines know that achieving something good takes time. And the best writers are fiercely critical of their own work.

'There are legions of lyrics that I kind of regret … "It's alarming how charming I feel." Coming from a Puerto Rican girl – what is she studying, Noel Coward?' Sondheim is regarded by many as the greatest living lyricist. Yet, in his eyes, he could have been so much better had he had the time to revisit and rewrite. You'll be a lot better, too, if you do the same.

Get a second opinion

Whenever possible, get someone to read what you've written. Do not, however, rush up to them and say: 'I've got to send this in 15 minutes, have a look and tell me what you think.' You're not giving them the information or time they need to give you a useful opinion.

If, for example, it's a document you're writing, explain who you are writing to, what the subject is, what your audience thinks about the subject at the moment and what you want them to think and do after they have read the document. Then give your critic enough time to read it thoroughly at least once. And, importantly, give yourself time to make any useful amends that they might suggest.

When it comes to brief writing, your line manager will, of course, be there to cast a constructively critical eye over your work. Indeed, they should always be on hand to help out if ever if you are stuck. If they aren't, remind them that a good manager always knows when their people have reached a 'love–40' moment and how to get them back to 'deuce'.

Once you've won the match point and the brief is ready to go into the creative department, here's a final suggestion that might save you quite a bit of time.

Some people think it's necessary to make the actual presentation of the brief into an event. They're afraid the creatives will otherwise be bored and won't want to work on the brief. So they take them out to the Serpentine and brief them on a rowing boat, or take them up the London Eye 250 feet above the Thames. Those who haven't got time for that might simply take the team to the pub.

Save yourself the time and effort. All any good creative team wants is a clear, well-written brief with a decent budget, a single-minded proposition and the time to do it justice.

If, however, they insist on being entertained, perhaps you should take them to the circus. And there you should leave them because they're obviously a couple of clowns.

Relevant abruption. Or what a big creative idea looks like

I f the chapter heading has tempted you to turn to this bit first, get back to the start. Go on, bugger off. You can't do the kind of effective creative you'll be proud of unless you do all the prep work I've described earlier.

For those, however, who've been with me from the start, here's a recap: to quote the immortal Howard Luck Gossage, 'People read what interests them, and sometimes it's an ad'. What interests them are the benefits you can bring them. More precisely, you need to show them that you can solve their problems with the products and services you are promoting.

The best work follows this problem/solution dynamic. More precisely, the best work comes from the best briefs, which clearly describe the problem/solution.

A good brief requires a big marketing idea, which essentially proceeds from the following pieces of information:

● What is the problem that is currently experienced by our customer/prospect?
● What is the solution provided by our client's product/service?

Quite simply, if the brief isn't right, the creative work won't be right either. Don't bother putting it into the team in the vain hope that they will crack it. They won't.

At best they will do something that might *look* right. The agency team will breathe a sigh of relief. The client might well be impressed. The work could even win an award. But it is highly unlikely that the customer/prospect will notice the work and engage with it in the way you want them to. Which means that by the only measure that matters, the work will have failed.

So I'll say it again. If the brief isn't right, the creative won't be either.

The purpose of a big creative idea …

If, however, the brief is right then all the team have to come up with is a big creative idea – one whose sole purpose is to dramatise or demonstrate the proposition.

They should know that there's no point presenting an idea that does anything else. However, it sometimes happens that the creative team find some information in the brief that doesn't directly relate to the proposition but which they think will make a better focus for their ideas. If so, explain that it is not their job to pick and choose which aspect of the brief they concentrate upon. Tell them what I've just told you: the big creative idea's sole purpose is to dramatise or demonstrate the proposition.

… and how to come up with one

What the team should be striving for is something called 'relevant abruption'.

What does this mean? Well, an abruption is a sudden and unexpected interruption. It breaks through the communications clutter and noise and gets your message noticed.

It is no good, however, if all it gains is your prospect's attention. For example, setting 'BULLSHIT' across a double-page spread in 36 point Frutiger Black will undoubtedly get you noticed. But unless you're actually in the agricultural fertiliser business, that ad won't make you much money. Indeed you'll just irritate your audience and, in turn, make them think less of the brand whose reputation you are trying to promote.

Your abruptive idea has got to be relevant, i.e. it must interrupt the prospect by drawing their attention to either the problem they are encountering or the solution that you are offering them. In short, it must lead them directly to the benefit they will enjoy after they've bought the product or service you're selling.

Anything else is irrelevant and should be rejected by the creative director when they are having the first work-in-progress meeting with the team.

If the idea is on brief, that's fine. Don't, however, make the mistake of thinking that all you need is an idea. You will also need to use your powers of persuasion.

Seize your opportunity and sell

I said in Chapter 1 that the main aims of all marketing communications are to help persuade your prospect that the product you're selling is better than the competition's product; and that it is in their interest to buy it.

Over the past 15 years, creatives have lost the confidence, ability or inclination to do this persuading. So nowadays, having fought hard to get the prospect's attention, the creative usually then concludes with something like: 'Now bugger off to our website and find out more for yourself.'

This is a lost opportunity because: (a) having just achieved the well-nigh impossible task of getting your prospect's attention you've just squandered the chance to sell; and (b) if your prospect does make the effort to go online they'll probably be frustrated because most websites are still painfully difficult to negotiate.

Prospects are, however, subjected to this 'drive to web' because of the agency and client's refusal to share information. Both the agency and client seem convinced that no one has the time to read their ads, mailpacks and emails any more.

Yet if you look at some of the most popular

sites on the web you'll see wall-to-wall copy. Take, for example, Procter and Gamble's www.homemadesimple.com. As Christopher Vollmer and Geoffrey Precourt explain in *Always On*: 'Its electronic pages are replete with contextually relevant content – product information, community stories, household ideas (recipes, decorating, tips for storing antiques) sweepstakes, promotions …'.

Don't be afraid to go into detail

Consumers would be just as happy to get this kind of information from other sources. Royal Mail recently commissioned the Future Foundation to research some of the most committed users of social networks. Over a third said they would welcome exclusive product news and that they'd be keen to see special offers. Sadly they are in the dark about what to buy, because marketing communications agencies are failing to communicate.

Yes, there are those smart agencies who are sending information packs to the group of customers who act as 'influencers' and then hope that they will WOM (word of mouth) on their behalf. But reliance on this kind of amplification alone is costing clients lots of money in missed revenue. This is made pretty obvious by a simple statistic from the Royal Mail's Home Shopping Tracker Study from 2007: the average online shopper spent £1,221 per year but this jumped to £1,526 for those who consulted

a catalogue before placing an order on the internet. Quite simply, the more information they had, the more confident they became and the more willing they were to buy.

So, while you have your prospect's attention, never forget that you are selling. There is an intelligent prospect at the end of every communication. Show how you can solve their problems. See the product through their eyes. Bring to life what it will do for them. Get them involved. Overcome their inertia and their scepticism. Use the facts that you'll find in the support points on the brief. And try to close the sale or get a response with a clear call to action.

Sounds reasonable? OK, that's enough theory.

Let's see the work

The examples here show the proposition (the big marketing idea) and then the way it was dramatised or demonstrated (the big creative idea).

The work I've chosen covers many of the media you'll have to work in. It also takes in the most common categories: business-to-consumer, business-to-business and charity marketing. As you'll see, I've also picked examples with pretty small budgets. Indeed, in most cases, I've focused on jobs that you wouldn't automatically assume might produce creative gems. Wherever possible, I've also given you the available results of each piece of work.

As you go through them you'll see that they share a couple of things in common.

First, they are rooted in the real world. Most bad creative (which means most creative) is a message to the consumer from the distant world of marketing. If you don't know what I mean, take a look at your TV, direct mail, inbox and magazines. Most of the creative might fascinate the client but it will be of no interest to the prospect. Try not to do work like this.

Instead, set your creative in the world in which the prospect lives. Use artefacts, messages from pop culture and references to their everyday lives. Indeed, just as the artists who followed Marcel Duchamp used ready-made and found objects and gave them new meaning with artistic spin, so you can do the same by giving these artefacts a commercial spin. If that sounds a bit arty-farty, bear with me. You'll see

what I mean and how effective it is.

Secondly, the production values of these examples are great. How many of your brilliant ideas never actually come out as you would like? Very few? Usually that's because the creative team haven't the time, budget or, let's be honest, the inclination to stay on the job right until it goes out of the door. And also the production department have neither the time, the money or the available expertise to do the job properly.

You can rectify this by: (a) reminding your creative teams of the last stage in James Webb Young's *A Technique for Producing Ideas*: 'shape and develop the idea for practical usefulness'; (b) hiring a head of production or creative services who will instil into their team a 'can do' spirit; and then (c) giving them all enough time to do their jobs properly.

OK, like I said, that's enough theory, here's the work.

Client
The AA

The brief

The AA is a roadside assistance service that rescues its members when their cars break down – which is the problem/solution in a nutshell. Drivers sign up annually and The AA has a mailing programme aimed at getting members to renew. The agency was asked to produce a final postcard that could be sent to those who'd ignored all other renewal mailings.

The proposition

If you don't renew your membership now, you're on your own if you break down.

The creative

The strongly branded front of the postcard carried the headline: 'Something to get you home if you don't restart your AA membership', plus a telephone call to action.

On the reverse, on brown cardboard, was a handwritten sign featuring the name of the home town of the recipient. For example, if that lapsing member was from London, the hand-written sign read 'LONDON'. If they were from Derby, the sign read 'DERBY' and so on. The message being, if they broke down once their membership had lapsed, their only option was to hitchhike home.

In most creative departments I doubt it there'd be a queue of people waiting to get their hands on this 'postcard' brief. Indeed, the temptation would be to just crack out the requisite 'postcard' in half a day and move on to more 'promising' assignments. You should not, however, follow this 'two-track' approach. Every brief is a chance to shine.

Another thing I'd mention is the effort that was put into the job after the idea has been bought.

Take a look at the hitchhiker sign for 'LONDON'. See the different shaped Os? Well, either Stephen Timms or Anthony Cliff, who were the creative team, had the presence of mind to realise you never make the same shape twice when writing by hand. So, to keep things real, they cut three different typefaces so there would never be any repetition.

It's the little things like this that really matter if you're trying, as I mentioned above, to get some reality into your advertising.

In fact, the achievement of verisimilitude is vital if you want your prospect to suspend disbelief long enough to engage with your message.

The front was strongly branded with a clear call to action.

The back was a hitchhiker's sign featuring the home town of the lapsed member.

Client
Papa John's

The brief

Papa John's have a chain of pizza parlours in Lima, Peru. All are situated downtown, which means their clientele are mainly passing trade who work, shop or socialise in the city. But what of the prospects who live outside the half-mile catchment area of each outlet? No matter how much they might have wanted one of Papa John's delicious pizzas, it was just too much of a hassle to go and get one.

The proposition

Call us and we'll deliver to your door.

The creative

The people who live in the more affluent suburbs of Lima are very security conscious and most have spy holes in their main doors so they can see who's visiting them before opening up. The agency realised this was an opportunity to give the prospect the Papa John's delivery experience before they'd even ordered by sticking a tiny image in front of the spy hole. This meant that the next time the door bell rang, the prospect would look through the spy hole and see what looked like the Papa John's delivery guy standing smiling outside with their pizza.

The results

Compared to the more conventional leaflet that had been dropped previously, this new approach saw an 80 per cent uplift in orders.

Once again, an unpromising low budget brief delivered a piece of effective and award-winning creative. Indeed, briefs don't come much less promising than those for that Cinderella medium, the doordrop.

Doordrops usually don't work because the lack of targeting means a lack of relevance. Moreover, they often fail because the team simply trot out the same old leaflet format.

That wasn't the case here. Instead of doordropping yet another leaflet, the team decided to do something that was truly abruptive and relevant. They used their local knowledge to create a format specific to the target audience. And, in so doing, got their message (and the phone number) right up there big and bold.

This is a great dramatisation of the benefit.

It also shows how a big creative idea can differentiate a 'me too' marketing idea. That's not to say it was a bad marketing idea.

As I explained in Chapter 4 when discussing propositions, sometimes it might be a benefit common to every product in the category. Then, as in this case, it's up to the creative team to – if you'll pardon the pun – deliver.

Agency
Quorum Nazca Saatchi & Saatchi, Lima

The agency stuck a tiny image in front of the door's security peep hole. So next time their doorbell rang, the prospect would see what looked like the Papa John's delivery guy standing smiling with his pizza.

Client
Honda

The brief

Many car owners and prospects had considered buying a diesel but decided against it because of the air and noise pollution problems associated with such engines.

The proposition

Here's a diesel engine that doesn't mess up the environment.

The creative

An animated cinema/TV commercial began in a beautiful natural paradise with the voice over: 'Here's a little song for anyone who's ever hated.' To the refrain 'Hate something, change something, make something better', paradise was suddenly lost as a noisy fleet of dirty diesel engines chugged across the skies, farting out fumes to the obvious disgust of the local ladybirds, bunny rabbits, toads, chickens, penguins and peacocks.

As the song continued ('We'd like to know, why it is so, that certain diesels must be slow and thwack and thum and pong and hum and clatter clat?'), one by one the engines were taken out by nature's vengeful creatures until none remained. Then, cued in by the lyrics 'Oh, isn't it just bliss when a diesel goes like this', a shiny, new, silent and clean engine appeared in the sky, riding the rainbow and joining the flamingoes and humming birds in a Busby Berkeleyesque spectacular which concluded with an aerial shot of the words 'Honda Diesel i-CTDi' picked out in a technicolour flower-bed, followed by Honda's logo and strapline: 'The Power of Dreams'.

The results

Sales of the diesel engine Honda Accord shot from 518 when the car was launched in 2003 to 21,766 in 2004 after the commercial aired. Brand awareness doubled in the three months following the campaign's debut and overall Honda sales increased by 35 per cent.

What you have here is one of the most critically acclaimed TV spots ever. What you also have is one of the best examples of a problem (prospects would buy a diesel but they thought they were dirty and noisy) and solution (Honda had created a diesel that was clean and silent).

It doesn't come a lot simpler or clearer than that.

Of course, what the creative team did with this simple and clear marketing idea was quite brilliant. To begin with, they did a car commercial that didn't even feature the car. But then again, why should the Accord be in there? The brief was all about the engine and certainly the team, with ruthless singularity of purpose, made the i-CTDi the star of the spectacular show.

And what a show. Like all great work, it was the product of incredible attention to detail. The animation took six months to perfect. The choice of voice over (Garrison Keillor) was inspired. As for the music, it was John Webster's belief that the tune accounted for 50 per cent of a commercial's success. And here is all the proof you'll ever need: I defy you to watch the commercial and not be whistling 'Can hate be good' for the rest of the day.

Agency
Wieden + Kennedy, London

The spot began in an unspoilt natural paradise which was invaded by a fleet of noisy, fume-farting diesel engines.

The animals fought back and started taking the diesels out. Then a brand new, clean and quiet engine appeared and took flight

along with the other creatures in a joyous spectacular culminating in the announcement of
the new i-CTDi engine and the appearance of the Honda logo.

Client
Amnesty International

The brief

Amnesty International defends prisoners of conscience. It does this by persuading individuals to protest to their own governments and to those governments who are abusing their citizens' human rights. The brief called for a rich media banner that dramatised the proposition that lies at the core of all Amnesty International's work.

The proposition

You can save an innocent life just by writing.

The creative

The first banner was an unbranded invitation to 'Play hangman'. Click on this and the game began (still unbranded). But what started as a game became a life and death struggle to find the three words in question that prevented the man from hanging. Those lifesaving words were 'Words save lives' and once the player found them the Amnesty logo appeared, along with a click-through to the website. Of course, if the prospect couldn't find the words in time, the poor man went to the gallows.

I've talked above the power of using bits of the real world in your work. Well, here's a great example using the universally familiar game, hangman. And how chillingly appropriate it was, too.

In Chapter 3 I also explained how charity work differs in that the problem is rarely experienced by the prospect but by a third party instead. Moreover, the solution is furnished not by the product or service but through the involvement of the prospect and their decision to give their time or money to the cause.

This is absolutely central to this piece of creative. Here the proposition was brilliantly dramatised as a race against time to find the right words before the man hanged.

It was also an excellent use of the medium. For this was digital at its involving best – drawing the prospect in and allowing them to participate in the drama until they themselves helped save the man, and in so doing, revealed the message.

Agency
Publicis Mojo, Auckland

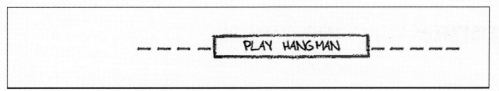

The first banner was an unbranded invitation to play hangman.

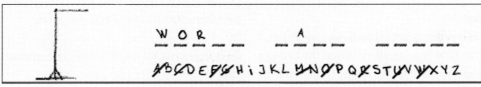

Having clicked, the 'game' began and became a

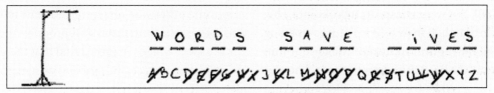

life and death struggle to find the words before

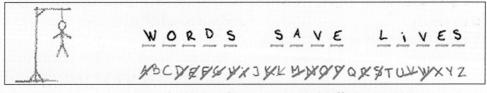

the man went to the gallows. If the player

got there in time, the Amnesty International logo

appeared with a click through to the website.

Client
Olympus

The brief
To persuade people who had just bought the Olympus mju 600 digital camera to also buy the PT-029 underwater case.

The proposition
Make sure you never miss out on that great underwater shot.

The creative
Each new Olympus mju 600 camera was shipped with a digital film pre-installed. When the camera was switched on for the first time, the film played on the screen. It showed a shark swimming ominously towards the camera, getting dangerously nearer and nearer until, as it was in close-up, it broke into a big smile. The film then froze as if a picture was being taken, and the caption appeared: 'Make your mju waterproof. The PT-029 underwater case.' This was followed by a call to action telling the prospect to order their case at the Olympus Emporium site.

The results
Over 10 per cent of those who bought the Olympus mju 600 went on to buy the PT-029 underwater case.

Here's a great example of a team inventing a medium in order to deliver their message at precisely the right time.

In fact, that makes it a great example of 'marketing at the moment of truth'. The theory of MATMOT goes like this: the great advertising pioneer Raymond Rubicam once said, 'Advertising is what you do when you can't send a salesman'. Problem is, whether it's direct mail, digital or TV, we often send our 'salesman' round at the worst possible time of day, i.e. when the prospect is busy thinking about anything but the problems that our products will solve.

So it pays to work out how you can communicate at that 'moment of truth'. That means: (a) when the prospect is actually experiencing the problem that your product or service deals with; or (b) the prospect is in some other way susceptible to your message; and (c) via a medium that is so appropriate that only the prospect will see it. (You'll find that these three points define a successful ambient campaign, too.)

In this case the prospect was wholly susceptible and the medium was totally appropriate. The prospect had just bought the Olympus. They were excited. They'd taken it out of the packaging. They'd started to point it at things. They'd pressed the button and, bingo, the shot of a lifetime had appeared on the screen. They weren't going to risk missing a shot like that for the sake of a few more euro on a waterproof case, were they?

Agency
Springer and Jacoby Werbeagentur, Hamburg

When the camera was turned on for the first time, a pre-installed film began to play
featuring a shark swimming ominously nearer.

As it came into close-up, it broke into a big smile. The film froze as if a picture was being taken and

the captions and call to action directed the prospect to the Olympus Emporium site.

Client
IBM Tivoli

The brief

To sell IBM's Tivoli software to IT directors in three different sectors: (a) retail and distribution; (b) financial services; and (c) public sector. Across all three sectors, the IT directors had a common problem: they felt that too much of their time was taken up with boring, routine jobs.

The proposition

Tivoli software will do all the routine jobs that keep you from doing more important things.

The creative

We dramatised this by actually packaging Tivoli as 'the invisible IT expert' – who could be bought off the shelf to come and do all the humdrum jobs in the department.

The results

We mailed 3,669. The total value of sales was £1,158,293, and the total cost of the mailing was £9,871. This gave an ROI of 117:1.

We've looked at work aimed at consumers. But what about business-to-business? Do those audiences respond to the same problem/solution dynamic? Of course they do. In fact, in a society where the majority of employees feel overworked, unappreciated and stressed to the limits of endurance, you should have little difficulty identifying the problems your clients' products can help solve.

In this case, the creative team dramatised the benefits of Tivoli software by personifying it as the guy who comes in and quietly takes care of all the time-consuming grunt jobs that otherwise monopolise the IT director's time.

This example is also interesting because it shows that individuals who share the same job title can experience the same problem but require slightly different outcomes from the solution. In retail and distribution, for example, the emphasis was on how Tivoli would increase overall productivity. In the public sector, however, the focus was on cost-cutting.

Tailoring the creative to fit the recipient begins with the brief. And while all three briefs shared the same proposition, the other sections in the brief varied according to the sector. This meant that the team could fine-tune the argument to the prospect – not only on the packaging that carried 'the invisible IT expert' but also in the two-page letters that accompanied it.

Two pages? Isn't that too much copy? Certainly not. Remember what I said at the start of this chapter about providing your prospect with the information that persuades them to buy your product? Well, in business-to-business, this is particularly important. First, because the purchase price is often very high. And second, because the person you are writing to is rarely the person who signs off that purchase. In this case, the IT manager would probably have had to go to the finance director for approval. They may also have had to compete with other colleagues for a slice of a limited budget. Therefore, it was vital to give them all the facts they'd need to win the argument.

Tivoli Software was positioned as 'The Invisible IT Expert' who would do all the routine jobs in the Retail and Distribution sector…

… the Finance sector…

… the Public Sector.

The back of the packaging provided fact filled case studies

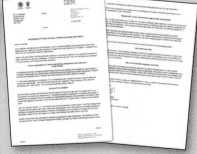
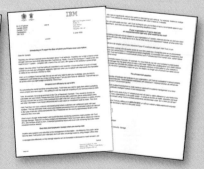

and the letters explained why each specific model was right for that particular sector.

Client
Xerox

The brief

Xerox asked us to launch the new Docucolor 2240 copier printer. In fact, they asked us for an idea that would get the Docucolor 2240 not just into the trade press but also into the national newspapers. Then they told us they had only £25,000 to spend.

The prospects' problem was clear: most people considered good colour copies to be too expensive. This led us to:

The proposition

Docucolor gives quality colour prints that everyone can afford.

The creative

We persuaded Gavin Turk, a leading Young British Artist, to create an original piece of art on a sheet of A4 paper.

We then arranged for him to appear for 45 minutes at the Tate Britain art gallery. There, he used a Docucolor 2240 to make colour prints of his original work, signed these prints and sold them – for just 10p, the price of a Docucolor 2240 print.

To get people to go to the Tate, we produced an ad that we ran in London's number-one listings guide, *Time Out*, and postcards targeted at trendy/art student bars. Then we contacted the press.

The results

Over 800 people queued for three hours to get a signed copy of the Gavin Turk original for just 10p. (Within three hours they were being sold on eBay for £95.) We were even paid a visit by a curious Sir Peter Blake, the father of modern art in the UK.

More importantly, photographers from the *Financial Times*, *Daily Telegraph*, *The Times* and *The Independent* covered the event. It was also previewed in the London *Evening Standard* and the *Metro*. Needless to say, the print and copier trade press were also there in force. Aside from getting the national press interested in a photocopier, the event itself generated 10 leads plus two sales – from Tate Britain.

Although the choice of medium was unorthodox, this is just another example of problem/solution and relevant abruption in action. Like all effective ideas, this one also delivered a clear demonstration and dramatisation of the proposition.

I should point out, however, that it would have been useless without the PR we generated. And if you're planning to create a 'happening' similar to the Gavin Turk event, then you need to start planning your PR coverage at the very earliest date. Indeed, give yourself time to create a press pack (like the one in the next case study) that can be sent out to journalists along with your press release.

To generate interest
we ran this ad in
Time Out magazine

and sent these postcards to journalists.

As a result, 800 people queued for hours for a 10p print from Gavin Turk …

… and we got pre-event coverage in the *London Evening Standard* and the *Metro*, and attracted journalists from *The Independent*,
The Times, the *Daily Telegraph* and the *Financial Times*.

Client
The National Phobics Society

The brief

The National Phobics Society (now called Anxiety UK) is the UK's leading charity for sufferers of obsessive compulsive disorder (OCD). When they came to us they had little money. So, instead of doing conventional creative work, we attempted to generate media coverage by inviting journalists to a news conference staged by the National Phobics Society.

One of the most common forms of OCD is the obsessive need for order. Sufferers must have everything neat and in its place. This was the insight that informed the press pack we sent out to journalists.

The proposition

We'd like you to write the inside story on obsessive compulsive disorder.

The creative

We sent journalists responsible for health-related issues a computer keyboard in a box. On the outside of the box was the line: 'We think it's time you wrote an article about Obsessive Compulsive Disorder.'

When the journalist opened the box they found the keyboard. On closer inspection they saw that all the keys had been rearranged from the standard QWERTYUIOP format to ABCDEFGHIJ … The line on the inside of the box read: 'But try writing it as a sufferer.' The copy underneath was, in effect, the press release. Note here the team's (obsessive?) attention to detail in that each paragraph began with the sequential letters of the alphabet. Thus, once again, mirroring the sufferer's need for order.

The results

From a budget of less than £3,000, 19 journalists attended the press conference, including those from the *Sunday Mirror*, *Daily Mail*, London City Radio and *Channel 4 News*. The National Phobics Society was covered in *The Times*, *The Sunday Times* and *The Independent*. Our PR work for the National Phobics Society also resulted in the BBC dedicating a 12-minute slot to both the charity and our marketing campaign during the prime-time network show *Inside Out*, which was commercial air time worth an estimated £400,000.

I said in the previous case study that you should start work on the press pack as soon as the creative idea's been had.

At HTW we were very keen on PR because: (a) people are more likely to believe a news story than they are a piece of marketing, and (b) as, in this case, we could get a small budget to go a very long way.

We also knew that a journalist's working life is one of either famine or feast. They have either too many stories to cover or none at all. So if your press release arrives at a time when they are gorging on news, it won't be noticed and it'll quickly be binned.

As you can see here, the trick is to cut through the clutter with a bit of relevant abruption and then to make sure you've sent something that stays on the journalist's desk long enough to be around when the news famine sets in.

To get journalists to write about Obsessive Compulsive Disorder, they were sent a keyboard.

But to reflect the OCD sufferer's need for order we rearranged the standard QWERTYUIOP format to ABCDEFGHIJ and on the Press Release (on the inside of the lid) we started each of the 26 short paragraphs with the next sequential letter from the alphabet.

Client
Macmillan Cancer Support

The brief

When cancer strikes, sufferers who claim benefits are often kept waiting months for their money to come through. Macmillan Cancer Support asked us to create an email inviting Members of Parliament to an all-party meeting at which Macmillan would begin lobbying for legislation to speed those payments along.

The proposition

Cancer sufferers can't afford to wait for their benefits.

The creative

We sent MPs an email about the new campaign Macmillan was launching. The email heavily implied that they'd better know about it in case their constituents asked for their view. When they clicked on the link they saw the familiar 'loading' wheel, which span for about ten seconds until a sequence of captions then explained how people suffering with cancer had to wait for months for their benefits and that some died not just in pain but in poverty. After the final caption, a page loaded that explained what the MP could do to help the campaign.

The results

Over 100 MPs attended the parliamentary launch of Macmillan Cancer Support's campaign for a better deal for those dealing with cancer.

Note those results. Over 100 MPs out of a total of 646. That's pretty amazing, given the fact that only on the rarest occasions is the House of Commons even a quarter full. It's clear to me why the email worked.

Earlier in this chapter I said you should never send people messages from the world of marketing because, frankly, your prospects aren't interested. Instead, you've got to send them bits of the real world and give them – in this case literally – a deft commercial spin. Well, this is a fine example of that argument in practice.

We've all stared at a site's loading wheel and, with growing frustration, wondered 'Is it actually loading?'

Here the prolonged spin of the loading wheel was our abruption. It held the recipient's attention long enough for them to get mildly irritated. Then its relevance became clear as the captions revealed the message and shamed the MPs into realising their own inconvenience was petty compared to the wait experienced by those fighting cancer.

Having got the message, the MPs were almost duty bound to go to the meeting. Thankfully, 100 or so MPs had that sense of duty and lent their support.

  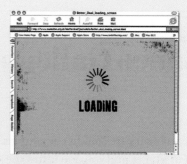

After the MP clicked the initial email, they saw only the loading wheel.

At the point of irritation, they were shown captions which explained the problems

faced by cancer patient's who were awaiting benefits

and the part the MP could now play in providing the solution.

Client
Banco Gallego

The brief

The problem here couldn't be simpler. If you've got a bit of money and you don't trust the stockmarket, you're constantly on the look out for the bank who can offer you the best rate of interest.

Banco Gallego solved the problem with a remarkable market-beating rate of 10 per cent. However, it only had a modest budget and was competing against much bigger, better-known banks.

The proposition

Get an amazing 10 per cent interest rate on your savings.

The creative

In June 2006 the TV sports commentator Julen Lopetegui collapsed while talking to camera. The recording of the faint spread through online streaming video sites like YouTube. However, nobody ever knew why Lopetegui had fainted. Then, four months later, unbranded press ads and posters appeared, which directed people to a website (www.whylopetegui fainted.com) and promised to reveal all.

Once at the site, viewers saw a video purporting to be a continuation of the filming of the incident. In the clip the camera filmed Lopetegui fainting and then pulled back to show the crew standing around perplexed. At the end of the clip viewers saw a crew member standing with a prompt card proclaiming Gallego's new 10 per cent deal. The inference being, it was this news that pole-axed Lopetegui.

A microsite explained the benefits of the new account and enabled users to forward the video on to friends. The teaser poster and press were then replaced by branded versions explaining the benefits of the account.

The results

Banco Gallego's 'Why Lopetegui fainted' video achieved over 14,000 registered viewings on YouTube, 43,435 site visits and 7,738 downloads from the website. Measured against the client's objectives, the campaign over-achieved new client acquisitions by 132 per cent and new deposits by 157 per cent.

This is a great example of off and online media working together to deliver a hugely effective, award-winning campaign.

As with the previous case study, it is also an object lesson in taking a part of the real world and spinning it slightly in order to get people interested in your message. The Lopetegui fainting video had already had over 500,000 views on the likes of YouTube and MySpace before the campaign began. So it was already a 'part of the real world'.

The agency, the brilliant creative powerhouse Shackleton Madrid, left nothing to chance. Note the intelligent use of the mixed media that teased and revealed. And then there was the graphic device, which reinforced the idea with a witty reference to the outstretched feet of the prone Lopetegui. And finally, let's not forget the client who had the vision to name the product 'Deposito Lopetegui'. That really did root the marketing of this product in the real world.

Agency
Shackleton, Madrid

Four months earlier, TV pundit Julen Lopetegui had fainted on camera. The unbranded press ads and posters directed people to the microsite that would explain why he fainted.

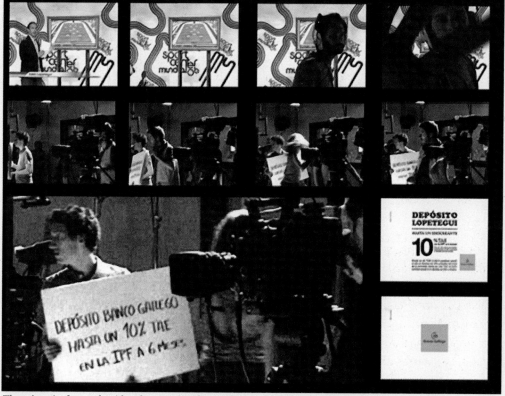

The microsite featured a video showing the aftermath of the incident. The crew stood around perplexed until finally the camera focused on a guy holding a cue card announcing Banco Gallego's 10 per cent deal.

Branded online and offline creative took up the story, explained the benefits of the account and generated leads.

How to build a brand and get response – the old way and the new

So far, most of the examples we've looked at have been tactical pieces of work that came from the kind of bread-and-butter briefs you get every day of the week.

Hopefully you'll have seen how the best creative can flourish in what might look like the least fertile ground. Moreover you'll have noticed how the problem/solution dynamic helps you devise the most potent propositions. And how, regardless of the medium, relevant abruption ensures that your work is seen and acted upon.

Now I'd like to take you through a couple of bigger, multimedia assignments. One of which took months to run and the other over five years.

Brand response: the secret of our success could be yours as well

Both of the cases I'm about to show you are examples of brand response. You may recall that in this book's very first paragraph I mentioned this term and its importance to the agency founded by me and my partners, Tim and Martin.

Brand response was the secret of our early success. Until then clients had had to go to an advertising agency for their brand-building communications and a

direct marketing agency for their sales and retention.

In most cases, the ad agency had only the vaguest inkling of what was working. And most direct marketing agencies knew nothing about brands. Often as not, the work they did contradicted the messages being delivered by the advertising and actually damaged the brand.

What we offered was an agency that understood that all marketing activity should proceed from a brand idea, and that every communication had to either refresh or reinforce the brand idea, while simultaneously driving response. As you can imagine, clients loved it.

Hopefully you'll see why from the first example I'm going to show you. It explains how to reposition a brand, build its equity and get a response at the same time, via a predominantly print campaign.

The focus on print should be useful to you, since you don't see many good, long-lasting and effective press and poster campaigns around at the moment.

> Every communication had to either refresh or reinforce the brand idea, while simultaneously driving response.

The second example takes us to where many believe the future of brand building and selling lies. You'll see how this kind of marketing uses Web 2.0 to something approaching its potential. And, of course, how it achieves this in a totally abruptive and relevant fashion.

But more of that later. Let's begin with our first lesson in brand response.

It comes from M&G Investments. Please don't turn off because this is financial services. You've just seen how that great Spanish agency, Shackleton Madrid, did wonderful work for a bank with their Lopetegui campaign.

Well, for over five years, the creative we did for M&G Investments delivered more awards for my agency than any other account. More pertinently, I'm pretty sure it is the only campaign that has won both an APG Creative Planning Award (concerned mainly with advertising strategy) and an Institute of Direct Marketing Business Performance Award (concerned primarily with direct response).

Incidentally, if you would like more background and results please consult either of the above organisations' published papers, as I have done for the following case study.

Client
M&G INVESTMENTS

The brief

In 2001 the M&G brand had lost its focus, fund performance was poor and response to its advertising was dwindling. Throughout 2001 M&G had raised its marketing expenditure by 48 per cent yet had seen spontaneous awareness drop by 9 per cent. It was against this background that M&G hired us to reposition their brand and arrest the decline.

There didn't appear to be a clear brand idea so our first task was to devise a new brand proposition. As with any proposition, the starting point had to be: 'What problem are we solving on behalf of the customer?'

The customer

In 2001 the customer was frightened. At the best of times investors are uncertain about the markets. But 2001 was actually then looking like 'the worst of times'. The stockmarket was tumbling down to new lows. The disintegration of American corporate giant Enron and the demise of Arthur Andersen, the collapse of Equitable Life and the scandal over pensions mis-selling caused panic and uncertainty that were only heightened by the terrorist attacks on the Twin Towers on September 11.

Research told us there was a clear need for a brand that allayed the investor's fears by providing open, detailed information about the investment market and investment products. We asked ourselves: 'Were the competition providing this guidance?'

The competition

The answer was 'No'. All the major players were reliant on a mnemonic – i.e. a symbol that would represent their brand and make it memorable among customers and prospects. For Scottish Widows this symbol was a woman in black, for Jupiter it was a big planet, for New Star an exploding galaxy, for Perpetual a mountain, for Fidelity a torch, etc.

With their reliance on these symbols, none of the major players actually told the consumer anything about the products they were selling and why they were right as an investment.

But could M&G step on to the high ground and be that voice of authority?

The research

Research told us 'Yes'. We spoke to the people who worked at M&G, we spoke to their customers and their prospects. Importantly, we also spoke to independent financial advisers (IFAs) who sold investment products.

They told us that, despite poor fund performance, M&G was still known for its 'integrity', 'durability' and 'straightforwardness'.

Put together, this sounded very much to us like 'trustworthy'. And in financial services in troubled times, there's no better thing to be than 'trusted'.

The brand idea

So, our brand idea became: 'The truth about investing as we see it.'

The Brand Book explained the work to the most important people of all: the M&G staff.

Before we did any advertising we explained this idea to the most important audience of all, the M&G staff. We knew it was vital that they understood and endorsed our thinking. So before the campaign broke we gave every one of them an M&G 'brand book', *Our Way*, which explained the current market and customer dynamics and introduced them to their new brand idea and the brand values that underpinned it.

It was well received by M&G staff. They thought it accurately reflected their approach to the customer. But who really was 'the customer'?

The target audience

We defined the target audience as people with assets of £30,000–£200,000 and/or an annual income of £30,000 plus. These 'mass affluents', however, included many people under the age of 45 who quite simply were not ready to invest. They had, for instance, high mortgage payments and children eating away at their disposable income.

The ones we identified as M&G's best prospects were older, empty-nesters, who had paid off their mortgage. We knew that some 80 per cent of the UK's disposable wealth was held by these over-50 'affluent silvers'. We also knew that most advertisers ignored them. We decided not to make that mistake.

At the start of Chapter 5 I noted how agencies and clients starve their prospects of information. Well, in this case, this was a particularly big mistake because we knew that these 'affluent silvers' were ravenous for product detail.

Indeed, it became apparent that they were characteristically incapable of making a spontaneous purchase.

And, when it came to their investments, who could blame them for being meticulous? Unlike 30 or 40-year olds, these people did not have the time left to recoup the losses of a bad investment decision. They had one last chance to secure a reasonably prosperous future.

Our research told us that, not surprisingly, they were willing to do *their* own research. Which meant they welcomed long copy.

So our advertising went into detail and explained such issues as:

- When is the best time to invest?
- How do you protect your investments in a volatile market?
- What is an ISA?
- When should you invest in a bond?
- What is a fund of funds?
- How do you get an income in retirement?

Choice of media
In this sector (and elsewhere) no one had done a long-copy campaign for years, so that approach was in itself abruptive. So, too, was the choice of media, for we did something no other investment house had attempted:

we ran full-page brand response ads not in the personal finance pages but in the body of such newspapers as *The Times, Daily Mail* and *Daily Telegraph.*

We also did something else that was different. We ran long-copy billboards. That's right, billboards with 800 words and a response element. The trick, however, was that we bought them on the Underground and at railway stations where we had a captive audience.

Brand response press and posters
If the style of advertising (long copy) and the media choice (full page, run of paper) was abruptive, so too were the headlines. For example, we launched with: 'In our opinion, there's never ever been a better time to invest in the stockmarket.' The poster had only been up for three hours when the BBC rang M&G to invite (or should I say challenge) the sales director to appear on *Newsnight* to explain exactly why he was running such a bullish headline at a time when

There were long copy posters aimed at captive audiences at railway and Underground stations.

In our opinion, there's never ever been a better time to invest in the stockmarket.*

At the moment, we believe the stockmarket is having the equivalent of a January sale.

Shares have fallen 13.3% in the last 12 months.

And, to us, it seems there are plenty of bargains to be had.

Others, however, might say you'd be throwing good money after bad.

Wouldn't you be better off selling your existing shares – before it's too late – and putting the money somewhere nice and safe, like a building society?

To answer these questions, we'll have to travel back to the dim (largely thanks to the regular blackouts and power cuts) and distant days of the early 'seventies.

Up to 58% off all stocks.

Back then, if you'd listened to popular opinion, the only thing you would have invested in was a candle factory.

The oil crisis in the Middle East caused share prices to plummet 58% in little over 12 months.

At that moment a lot of people were scrambling to get out of the market. A few people, however, were actually looking not just to stay put but to buy more.

How clever.

Within 12 months, the market had bounced back and risen by 154%. And if you'd had the foresight to invest £1,000 when the market was at its lowest, you'd have increased your money to £2,540 in little over 12 months.

*If you don't count December 1973 that is.**

Remember Ted Heath? Three-day weeks? Power cuts? Back then, the stockmarket plummeted to an all-time low – thanks to an unexpected rise in oil prices. But within two years, it had regained its original value and continued to rise.

**Or 1914–18, 1929, 1939–45 and, perhaps, 19 October 1987.

But what of the people who took their money and put it in a building society?

Well, they'd have known it was perfectly safe and secure.

However, that very same £1,000 would have only grown to £1,077 in the same period.

In case you're wondering who we are.

We introduced the UK's first unit trust on St George's Day, 23 April, 1931.

We successfully lobbied for regulation of the industry back in 1939 – which is why you can trust unit trusts.

In 1954, we introduced the UK's first regular savings plan, in which you could invest just five shillings a week.

In 1971, we became the first UK fund manager to invest in international markets.

We launched the UK's first pure corporate and high yield corporate bond funds.

We introduced the UK's first no initial charge PEP.

M&G Investment Management are one of the largest investors in corporate bonds in the UK.

We manage investments for 344,505 individuals in the UK.

M&G Investment Management currently looks after £111,975,000,000 worth of investments – make that £111,975,001,526.

Of course, after the events of 1974, the stockmarket bounced back even stronger (as it had after the First World War, the crash of 1929 and the Second World War) and continued to rise.

Until 19 October 1987....

20% off everything. For one day only.

Black Monday.

In 48 hours, share prices turned from green to red around the world.

The FTSE All Share fell 20%. The Dow Jones slumped 18%. And the Nikkei dropped 17%.

Another great day for bargain hunters – especially as, you guessed it, the market went on to make a full recovery and bounce back even stronger.

Which brings us up to today.

Bargain hunters beware.

If you look at the chart opposite, you'll see you can snap up shares in a lot of famous names for a fraction of the price you'd have paid just a few months ago.

However, it pays to shop around and, when you consider there are over 800 companies listed on the stockmarket, it takes a lot of expertise and effort to emerge with the very best deals.

While it can be exhilarating fun trying to do this yourself there are less dangerous hobbies, such as running the bulls at Pamplona, that you might take up.

So what should you do?

Get a team of specialists working for you.

It costs you from as little as 1% of your investment a year in management charges to have some of the most experienced fund managers in the world working on your behalf.

And, at M&G for example, not only do you get the fund managers. There are analysts and researchers checking out not just the best deals but also the most lucrative prospects.

Every year we scrutinise over 1,000 companies. And every one of the FTSE 350 companies is investigated closely, their senior executives being grilled on business strategy and how they intend to achieve it.

Depending on the size of your investment, all this can cost you just a few pounds a month.

Which, some might say, is a bit of a bargain in itself.

Buy now, while stocks last.

As we keep saying, compared to prices just a few months ago, there are great savings to be made on the stockmarket.

The secret of investing is the same as the secret of good comedy – timing.

Get this right, and you could be laughing all the way to the bank.

The secret lies in what the experts call 'buying at the bottom.' And there are some who think that moment has already past.

We ourselves believe the recovery will happen sooner rather than later.

Which is why, if you don't count 1914–1918, 1929, 1939–1945, 1973 and, perhaps, 19 October 1987, we reckon there's never been a better time to invest in the stockmarket.

If you'd like to know more about how you might capitalise on the current uncertainty in the markets, please get in touch.

We'll send you our free Guide to Investing.

Just call free on 0800 072 6146 quoting reference XXX (lines are open 8.00am to 8.00pm, seven days a week), or complete and return the coupon below. Or visit www.mandg.co.uk

If you prefer, please ask your IFA about us and how we could help you.

Some of this week's special offers.

	Was	Now
Cable & Wireless	1022p	311p
Royal Doulton	70½p	12¾p
Marconi	800p	9½p
Redwane	163½p	1p

These were correct when we went to print on 23/01/01. But they've probably gone up and down since then.

Please send me a copy of your Guide to Investing.

Name: _____

Address: _____

Postcode: _____

Email: _____

Tel. No: _____

Are you an existing M&G customer? Yes □ ref. XXXX No □ ref. XXXX

Please return to: The M&G Group, FREEPOST 5131 (There, you're 27p better off already). Chelmsford, CM1 1FB.

M&G may use your information for marketing purposes and to any clients your information to our service providers and other members of the Prudential Group. The transfer of this information will be restricted at all times. If you do not wish to be included in our marketing programmes, please tick the appropriate boxes. By post □ by telephone □ by email □. You have the right to ask for a copy of the information we may hold about you.

This was the launch ad which ran when the FTSE 100 was around 3200 – the lowest for 20 years. The BBC promptly rang and invited M&G to explain themselves on *Newsnight*.

the markets were crashing.

This was perfect, because M&G's target audience was precisely the kind of people who tuned into BBC2's *Newsnight* programme. It gave M&G hundreds of thousands of pounds worth of free air time – and a lot of credibility.

Tone of voice

Our target audience loved the ads. Many wrote in to say how much they appreciated the information that M&G was offering them.

They also liked the tone of voice. As you'll see, it was written in an informal fashion as if we were sitting opposite the prospect talking with them. Of course, we never lost sight of who that prospect was – aged 50 plus and very much a product of middle England.

In one ad we suggested 'Go and get yourself a cappuccino'. I'm afraid this went down badly, as this was not the Starbucks generation. When we changed it to 'cup of tea' they were a lot happier.

The look of the ads

As I said, they liked the long copy. Indeed, those wall-to-wall words were a design element that actually became a mnemonic for M&G. Over time, they were as instantly recognisable as Jupiter's planet and Scottish Widows' woman in black. The important thing was that the copy-heavy mnemonic communicated the fact that M&G was knowledgeable and ever-willing to share its wealth of information. Which was entirely consistent with and reinforcing of the brand positioning.

Our audience also liked the layout. We purposely chose what might be described as an old-fashioned serif typeface for headlines (Fournier) and for body copy (Mrs Eaves) because they were ungimmicky and easy on the eye for an older audience who might have trouble reading. We made reading easier still by breaking up the copy with useful cross-heads. These helped us tell the story at a glance and allowed the reader a variety of ways of entering the ad.

Another way into the ad was via the vignettes we created. These were captioned illustrations or photographs of actors, TV personalities and sportsmen/women from 20 or 30 years ago. We chose them carefully because we wanted our target audience – and them alone – to recognise these figures. It was, in effect, our way of saying 'This ad's for you'.

Of course, the best way of saying 'This ad's for you' was by making it interesting to the target. And once again it was the problem/solution dynamic that helped us achieve this.

Each ad had a dual purpose. The strategic purpose was to reinforce and refresh the brand idea: 'The truth about investing as we see it.' The general problem of confusion about the investment market and products still had to be overcome and each ad had to say that M&G could be trusted to provide the necessary clarity. There was also a secondary tactical purpose for each

For five years M&G ads demystified the markets and explained investment products,

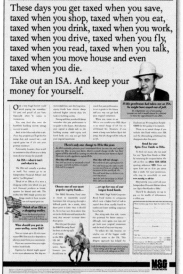

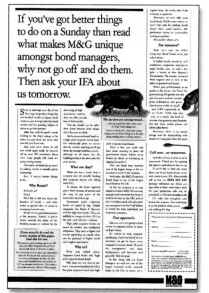

and solved the problems of an over 50s audience who were hungry for information.

99

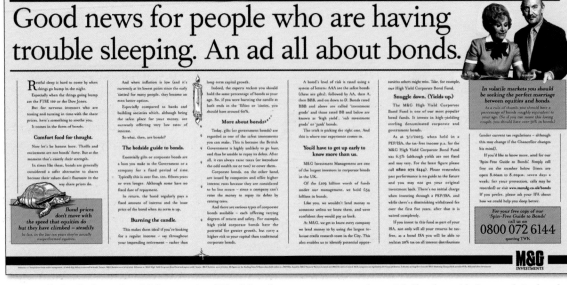

We regularly asked ourselves this key question, 'What's keeping our customers awake at night?' and provided a remedy in the ads.

ad or campaign. Here the problem would be a current issue that was weighing heavily on our prospects' minds. To identify it, we would meet regularly with the CEO and the sales and marketing directors of M&G and set ourselves the question: 'What's keeping our customers and prospects awake at night?' As you can see, one of our headlines actually began: 'Good news for people who are having trouble sleeping …'.

Brand response product ads

So, the brand response press and posters discussed the issues that were troubling our prospects – and then introduced an investment vehicle and an M&G product that might help.

Our product ads were more direct and sold a lot harder. They were aimed at people actively searching for an investment product and, as such, were

Product ads were more direct but still had that friendly, informative tone.

placed in the personal finance pages of the newspaper.

However, true to our brand idea, these ads clearly explained what the product was and how it worked. This was unusual, as most of the competition simply ran their past performance figures big and bold and hoped that might do the trick.

Brand response channel ads to independent financial advisers

Our channel ads were, of course, also informed by the brand idea – 'The truth about investing as we see it' – and spoke to independent financial advisers with the same authoritative voice.

Here, too, we took a point of view and presented it clearly. Sometimes even to the point of questioning the conventional wisdom of the time.

We did, however, accept that IFAs were not as willing to read all our long copy, so we introduced an at-a-glance key-selling-points section that the IFA could use when discussing M&G's products with a client.

Of course, we did so much more than just press and posters. For maximum impact, we dovetailed our print campaigns with emails, direct mail, inserts and radio. We introduced customer magazines, which were great for cross-selling and upselling. And for fulfilment we produced numerous *Spin-Free Guides*, which explained M&G's products in simple, jargon-free terms. Indeed, as you'd expect, everything we did was designed and written in M&G's characteristic style and tone of voice.

The results

As a direct result of the repositioning campaign, in the first six months of the year (which includes the vital ISA-selling season of January–April) the total response was up 32.5 per cent while media spend was down 31.7 per cent. This gave a reduction in cost per enquiry of 53.9 per cent.

In those crucial ISA selling months of January–April, total sales increased by 15.3 per cent and ISA sales by 19 per cent. (Internet sales to the 'silver surfers' increased by 38 per cent.) This meant that the total cost of acquiring a customer as a percentage of sales fell by 35 per cent.

The channel ads spoke with the same authoritative voice.

By the end of the April, M&G's total market share was up 14.3 per cent, with its market share in ISAs and PEPs up 24.8 per cent.

And all this was achieved in a dramatically shrinking market: across the industry direct sales to the customer were down 30 per cent and sales via IFAs were down a similar amount. Likewise, customers of other investment houses were rushing to withdraw their money and customer redemptions were rising by 25–30 per cent. At M&G, however, customer confidence remained strong. In fact, during this period, M&G's customer redemptions actually *fell* 19 per cent.

This was the impact of the brand response campaign after 12 months. Results remained robust as each new customer campaign rolled out. But if the campaign delivered response, what of its effect on the brand?

For the long-term results, let's look at research taken four years after the campaign was launched:

In brand tracking, M&G was ranked number one above all competitors on these crucial criteria:

- 'A company you can trust.'
- 'Has proven track record.'
- 'Appropriate for substantial wealth.'
- 'Offers a broad range of products and investments.'
- 'Has a strong, long-lasting brand.'

Such results prove the efficacy of brand response. Yet, in all honesty, the process by which we repositioned the M&G brand and produced the five years' work you've just seen differed little from that which led us to the proposition on the smaller tactical jobs I described in the last chapter.

All revolved around: (a) a marketing idea that identified the prospect's problem; (b) the solution provided by the client's product or service; and (c) a creative idea that dramatised or demonstrated this in an abruptive and relevant fashion.

So much then for the print-based approach to repositioning, brand building and response generation. Now let's have a look at what you can do with digital in the media mix.

Is this the future of brand response?

To my mind, and that of many people who are smarter than me, the most interesting work at the moment involves storytelling. Done properly, it begins with a problem-solving customer proposition, which is then, quite literally, dramatised through an episodic narrative.

If that sounds a bit high-faluting, basically this is usually the kind of thing you'll see: the story might begin with a film that is seeded on the net. Prospects get interested, look out for the next one, seek out the video blog, watch the webcast, sign up for a podcast, pass them on to their friends, go to the website, play

their own part in the drama, buy into the brand and, ultimately, the product.

Unlike all other media campaigns, the whole thing develops right there in front of the prospect. And done properly (and I'm not sure that this bit has yet been done 'properly') these campaigns actually allow the prospect to determine the development and direction of the creative. This gives the campaigns an immediacy and an authenticity unlike any TV, radio, press, poster or direct campaign that you've ever seen.

Actually that is not true. In fact, let me point you in the direction of the man who foresaw all this a long time ago.

Meet the man who saw all this coming over 40 years ago

I referred to him earlier and his name was Howard Luck Gossage. Here he is, in *The Book of Gossage*, describing his approach to writing a press campaign:

'We do one ad at a time. Literally that's the way we do it. We do one advertisement and then wait to see what happens; and then we do another advertisement. Oh sometimes we get way ahead and do three. But when we do, we often have to change the third one before it runs. Because if you put out an advertisement that creates activity, or response, or involves the audience, you will find that something happens that changes the character of the succeeding ads. It's like a conversation. You say something and then the other person says something; and unless you're a bore, you listen to what they say and respond accordingly.'

If you've never seen Gossage's work then put this book down, Google or eBay *The Book of Gossage*, buy it, read what he has to say about involving his audience, and look at his campaigns for Fina Petrol, Eagle Shirts, Qantas and Rainier Ale. Then make him your hero.

The inspiration behind the world's most respected agency

That is what the creative director of the world's most respected ad agency has done. Here is Alex Bogusky of Crispin Porter + Bogusky (CPB) talking to *New Media Age*:

'A huge hero of mine is Howard Gossage who was an advertising guy in the San Francisco area in the 1950s and 1960s. He would use coupons to create conversations with consumers. To me that's what you want to look at with any new technologies. You look at it as offering potential places where it is easier to have really rich conversations with consumers, and stop really thinking about media so much. Instead, think about relationships and the conversation and what you want that to be. Gossage would have gone completely bananas with the web.'

If you want to see Alex's take on the Gossage approach, then look up CP+B's great campaign for Coke Zero.

Alex Bogusky of CP+B is a huge fan of Gossage's conversational approach.

Everyone who is on a diet knows that they should drink low-cal drinks. They also know these drinks taste horrible. That's their problem. The solution? Well, let's see how CP+B set about convincing a sceptical public that Coke Zero actually did taste just like regular Coke.

The story that dramatised this began with two 'executives' from Coke's marketing department visiting a number of lawyers. They wanted to know if they could start legal proceedings against Coke Zero for 'taste infringement'. Their hilarious attempts to sue their own company were filmed secretly and then broadcast on and offline. Thereafter there were press ads and posters, viral videos, rich media banners and a website with a handy tool with which you could sue your friends for their own forays into 'taste infringement'.

The buzz was, as you might imagine, deafening. And once it subsided what was left was a once sceptical public who now knew that Coke Zero tasted identical to 'the real thing'. Story told. Message delivered. Problem solved.

Transporting a pub from New Zealand and London is pretty abruptive

Another good example comes from Publicis Mojo in Auckland, New Zealand. Their brief was to bring a bit of modernity and energy to Speight's beer - a traditional and quintessential Kiwi brand, whilst reinforcing the core values of mateship and loyalty that are a key part of Speight's identity.

Well, apparently an expat had written to Speight's from England. He wasn't necessarily homesick, just sick of the beer in London. So, he wondered, could they send him a crate of his favourite Kiwi beer?

Speight's went one better than that and blew the whole of the brand's annual marketing budget

A live weblog kept everyone updated on the 12,000 mile voyage and got 1,000 visitors a day.

building the young man a Speight's Ale House, mounting it on a container ship and sailing it 12,000 miles so he could have a proper pint in London. Which, by any standard, is pretty abruptive and very relevant to the brand positioning.

Of course, the expedition needed some shipmates and the newspaper recruitment ads got thousands of responses and generated lots of publicity. The media stuck with the idea as the five-man crew sailed across the Pacific, through the Panama Canal, via New York and eventually to dear old Blighty.

There were weekly updates on prime-time TV, regular radio reports and a live weblog, which got 1,000 unique visitors every day. By the time the boat sailed up the Thames, something like $2.5 million worth of PR coverage had been generated. Simultaneously, sales had risen by 6.5 per cent (in an otherwise declining market).

Perhaps more importantly, Speight's had achieved a 3 per cent increase in its share of 'beer adorers' – those extremely valuable (and thirsty) customers who generally account for 75 per cent of a beer brand's sales volume. Either way it had emphatically reinforced both its positioning and its position as New Zealand's No 1 beer brand.

Client
Volkswagen Golf

Here's one last example and the one I like best, because quite simply the hard results (sales leads) seem stronger. It comes from DDB Germany, who were briefed to boost sales and refresh the Volkswagen Golf's position as 'the people's car'.

Of course, they could have spent millions of euros on TV commercials, posters, press, radio, banners, MPUs and direct mail in a conventional multimedia campaign. But they did something smarter. They told stories about a character called Horst Schlämmer – a much-loved German 'everyman' and the perfect hero for a campaign aimed at reviving Golf's populist image.

As 'Schlämmer's quest' began, however, no one knew that VW was involved. For it kicked off online with Schlämmer announcing on his video blog that if he was ever going to be attractive to the ladies then it was about time he learned to drive.

Week after week, more and more people followed his genuinely funny adventures as he chose (and immediately crashed) his first car (a BMW) and took perilously to the road. The main platform was his video blog, accompanied by podcasts distributed through video-sharing sites like YouTube. There was also, by the end of the campaign, a documentary website.

It was only after several weeks that Volkswagen revealed itself as the sponsor of the whole promotion – and by then the German public was hooked. Indeed, three weeks later, when Horst finally took and passed his driving test, the nation shared his moment of triumph.

In just two months there had been 4,270,000 page impressions and 4,730,000 video downloads, making this the most viewed online video in Germany. Better still, Horst also headed the iTunes podcast charts and was number two in the blogscout charts as well.

The campaign kicked off online with Horst Schlämmer's unbranded video blogs.

Fans followed 'Schlämmer's quest' on YouTube.

Hundreds of thousands went to his documentary website.

TV, press and online news created even more interest.

Direct Mail targeted prospects and drove response.

While the VW website started some, not so serious, serious selling.

Agency
DDB, Berlin

One of VW's most lucrative campaigns ever

In most of those films the people were seeing Horst driving a Volkswagen Golf. And on the great day when Horst passed his test, he did so in what had, through association, once more become 'the people's car'. Moreover, by then 'Schlämmer's quest' had generated 90,000 qualified leads, of which 12 per cent were converted, which made this campaign one of the most lucrative in VW's illustrious marketing history.

It is, in short, a great example of how to refresh a brand and get response simultaneously.

As someone who had a hand in introducing the idea of brand response, I'm delighted to see it done in such ingenious fashion. For a few years now, I've felt that brand response's potential has yet to be realised. The idea had been popular for a while. Agencies said they were able to build brands and get response with the same communication. Few, however, had the necessary skills, and when the next big thing came along they were distracted.

That 'next big thing' was digital. And it seems appropriate now that the idea that replaced brand response might well be the one that brings it to fruition.

Interestingly, it's the ad agencies (like CP+B, Publicis Mojo and DDB Germany above) who are doing most of the best work. Why? Because, quite simply, they've always known that their communications are rooted

in the brand. If direct and digital agencies are to match them, then they need the same discipline.

It shouldn't be too difficult. All that's required is a brand idea born out of a problem and a solution. And an abruptive story idea that gets it noticed and is relevant enough for people to want to follow each episode as it develops. Then, like I said, the real trick will be to follow Gossage's advice and allow the prospect to determine the course your story takes.

The examples I've shown might not have done the last bit too well, but there have been encouraging signs from series like Diesel's *The Heidis*, the Ford-sponsored *Where are the Joneses?* and other webisodic shows that ask for such interaction.

And who knows, by the time you're reading this, there might also be some examples of the interrelated, multi-platform brand stories that McCann Erickson New York's chief technology strategist, Faris Jacob, calls 'transmedia narratives'. I certainly hope so, provided that each of those narratives helps dramatise or demonstrate the brand idea and generate response. I also hope you've done one of them.

But if that's the case then let's not get ahead of ourselves. Because this idea you've created still has one big hurdle to get over. Before it goes out into the world to grab your prospect's attention, it has to gain your client's approval. So let's follow the work out of the creative department and round to the client's office to look at how you go about selling it.

How to sell creative work

I f you've worked in the industry for a few years you'll have attended internal meetings that go something like this. The work is on the wall and everyone's happy. The account handlers are confident it will meet the client's objectives. The planner is sure it will 'resonate' with the target audience. The creatives are already online checking out BA's lunchtime schedule to Cannes. All is ticketyboo, when a junior exec asks: 'Who's going to present it?'

The copywriter looks up from the BA website and replies, 'Good work sells itself'. The senior account man nods knowingly and says, 'I think we'll let the advertising speak'.

At which point you might as well take the work off the wall, fold it neatly and toss it in the recycling bin. Because if the advertising *could* speak it would say: 'You idle sods. If you don't work out your sales pitch now, there isn't a snowball in hell's chance of me ever running.' And you know something, the ad would be right. Here's why.

If you want to hide in a forest, dress as a tree

Once clients know the creative process is under way, they start to anticipate the result. Now, they could spend five seconds pondering the outcome or five hours, but ponder they will. And in many cases their expectations will be conditioned by what they see being done in the sector.

In automotive, for example, they might imagine a car entering a tunnel at speed on the French Riviera's treacherous winding Grande Corniche. In financial services another cliché might spring to mind: that of the maze; or perhaps, that old friend, the needle in the haystack.

Alternatively the client will take as their guide the creative work done by the market leader, in the misguided view that if they, too, did work like that then they might have a chance of toppling the existing number one.

Whatever the image that pops into their head, you can bet it will be pretty conventional. And they will be expecting your creative work to look like everyone else's. This doesn't make for arresting work. As the saying goes: if you want to hide in a forest, dress as a tree.

Indeed, as we've seen in the last two chapters, the most arresting and effective work (from a hitchhiker's cardboard sign to a multinational corporation suing itself) is pretty unconventional. And when the client claps eyes on your unconventional work they'll be pretty surprised and then uncomfortable and then a little frightened. Which, in turn, means you're going to be disappointed, because without a great sales presentation they're not going to buy your big creative idea.

So, what makes for a great sales technique?

If you want to be able to sell, it certainly helps if you have a good relationship with your client. But you've got to be careful about the basis of that relationship. It is tempting to build it around your understanding of the politics of your client's company. This, however, is primarily a survival strategy. Frequently it leads to you becoming the client's representative to the agency as opposed to the agency's representative to the client. And you will never sell good work that deviates from the norm if you are the client's mouthpiece, because you'll always err on the side of caution.

You might, alternatively, base your relationship upon your social skills. Indeed, you can make your client like you by buying them lunch and drinks, and telling the most hilarious jokes. But the client is no fool and when they realise they're bankrolling this bonhomie they'll turn round and tell you that if they wanted new friends they'd go to a dating agency not an advertising, direct or digital agency.

No, the best way to sell (and the best way to build a good relationship) is to win their respect. And they will respect you most if they think you know more than they do.

Good? Bad? It's all a matter of opinion isn't it?

Winning their respect is crucial because one day, sooner or later, you'll present work to them that makes them nervous. They'll look at it in silence, suck their teeth and then tell you they won't be running the work.

Of course you'll try to persuade them of the work's greatness. And at that point they'll turn round to you and say: 'Yeah but what is "good" and what is "bad" is all subjective. You think it's great and I'm afraid that I don't. It's all a matter of opinion, isn't it?'

> The best way to sell is to win their respect. And they will respect you most if they think you know more than they do.

And yes, they're right, of course. It is all a matter of opinion.

But what they've got to realise is this: there are two types of opinion. The first is informed by both the historical context and the business context in which the work has been produced. Which is where you should be coming from.

The second type of opinion is informed by nothing more than the personal preferences and prejudices of the individual concerned. And this is probably where the client is coming from.

Let's start with their lack of historical context.

Would you ask someone who only eats at McDonald's to recommend a good restaurant?

Few clients can identify great work from the past. Even fewer are able to explain what makes one piece of classic creative better than the run-of-the-mill stuff. And one or two don't even know why such knowledge might be important. If that's the case with your clients, here's what you should ask them.

Suppose they're organising an important business dinner and need a suitable restaurant, whose advice would they take: the gourmand who has dined everywhere from the best bijou bistros to Michelin-starred restaurants, or the chap who prefers fast food and can venture a reliable opinion only on the relative merits of the Big Mac or the Double Whopper?

The sad fact is, in real life, our figurative fan of fast food is the man who commissioned the junk mail you received this morning. And you'll find his brand of blissful ignorance characterises a lot of client organisations (and, I'm afraid, most agencies, too). For, as Alan Tapp, Professor of Marketing at Bristol Business School says: 'There's a strong anti-learning culture in the UK. It isn't "cool" to have expertise or historical context.'

So if it's a case of 'don't know much about history', then how about the business context?

Well, let's face it, it's pretty difficult getting a firm grasp on your subject if you never stay in one place long enough. To quote another eminent academic, Hugh Davidson, Visiting Professor of Marketing at Cranfield School of Management: 'It has been a disease of marketers for decades that they think that if they have not been headhunted into a new job every 18 months they have failed.'

It wouldn't be so bad if they moved exclusively within, say, financial services or fast-moving consumer goods, and took their accumulated specialist wisdom from job to job. But instead they hop from sector to sector in a way best parodied by this fictional press release from Jeremy Bullmore's *More Bull*: 'Anglo-Galvanized announce the appointment of Clive Thrust as marketing manager, Aggregates. He has previously held similar positions with Scottish Widows, Pedigree

Petfoods, Rentokill and the Bristol Zoo.'

Of course, there is an argument for bringing knowledge and experience from other sectors. But it needs to be based upon a deep-seated understanding of the product, customer and market in question. And the lack of that means that good work doesn't always get bought.

At which point you can either curse the client for their lack of vision or you can start seeing the world through their eyes. Their job has changed beyond all recognition over the past few years, and the ever-increasing demands on their time mean that commissioning successful creative work is just one of a dozen tasks on their job spec.

If, as a consequence, they can no longer be the experts in marketing communications then you'd better make sure that you are. Which brings me back to selling and why the best way to sell is to convince your clients that you do, in fact, have a firm grasp of the knowledge they lack. That they can rely on that knowledge. And that your opinion is, indeed, valuable and, when it comes to the crunch, worth deferring to.

There are five areas of knowledge that you must master if you are going to sell your work.

1 Knowledge of marketing communications

If your client has little historical context then, as I said above, you've got to convince them that they can rely on yours. This means you have got to know things like this:

- What is a USP and who popularised the theory?
- What did the first banner ad say, when did it appear and who was it for?
- Who, in the 1960s, introduced the role of the account planner?
- How long should a direct mail letter be?
- What would be an example of a 'tipping point'?
- How would you define ambient advertising?
- What is the best viral campaign you've ever seen?
- What is an A/B split?
- What is the Pareto Principle as applied to patterns of consumption?
- Why should Web 2.0 and the semantic web be the engine of CRM?
- What is permission marketing?
- What is the purpose of a creative idea?
- Who wrote *Positioning*?
- What was *Lemon*?

The first ever banner ad: less than 16 years old, yet it's as obscure as Aramaic to most people in the industry.

If you can't venture a viewpoint on or an answer to any of the above, then your client is probably right to dismiss your opinion. In which case, I'd suggest you take another look at this book as you'll find over half the answers in here. And then try getting hold of the books I mentioned at the end of Chapter 1. As I said, read them and you'll suddenly become one of the most knowledgeable people in the industry.

If you've got some of the answers already, then start to show off your knowledge to your client. One thing you can do is get them into the agency and give them a brief illustrated history of the industry over a glass or two of wine. Position it as a review of the thinking that inspires your agency.

Lock everyone in the room until you all agree on what makes a good piece of work

Better still, get the client in for a 'good ad/bad ad' session in which they're encouraged to bring work and explain what they do and do not like about it. While you're sorting out the wheat from the chaff, explain the basics of what makes a good piece of marketing communication.

You'll find that this might be news to even your most senior of clients. So take this opportunity to share your knowledge and don't wait until you're presenting because by then it might be too late. I remember I was once trying to sell a press campaign to a marketing director who stared at the work in obvious discomfort. When I asked

her to share the problem with everyone, she said 'It's the headline. My eyes keep being drawn to the headline.' It would have been funny had she not blown out the entire campaign because she was afraid the headline was *too* compelling.

Use the work they've picked to make your points. Invariably the majority of the bad work will be confused, vague and free of any discernible benefit.

The good work will be a clear dramatisation of a problem/solution. Congratulate them on their fine judgement and then use the good examples as a means of explaining the importance of:

- the brief
- the focus on problem/solution
- the value of a single-minded proposition
- the power of an idea that dramatises the consumer benefit
- the need for enough time to bring it all together properly.

Impress upon them the fact that good, effective work will only come from such things. In fact, don't let them leave the room until you've all committed to building the creative process round all the points above.

Over time, the effect of that half-day in your office will fade. So maintain the offensive by impressing your client with your knowledge and enthusiasm. When you're in a taxi with the client, ask them about the ads they like that are currently on the TV and use the discussion to reinforce best practice. If you're at lunch with them, raise an issue that is currently being discussed in the trade papers and share your view. When you are waiting for a meeting to begin, strike up a conversation about a particularly good website you've visited recently. Explain why you were impressed and ask your client's opinion. Email your client articles you think they might find useful. Send them ads, mailings, URLs and blogs that are relevant to them. In short, leave them in no doubt that you have a thoroughly professional grasp of your subject.

Would you go to court with a barrister who winged it?

By this point, you might be wondering if all this hard work is necessary. Well suppose, for instance, that you're due in court and need a barrister to defend you. Would you hire one who, instead of studying your case and then citing precedent, preferred to bumble through in the hope of winning the jury over with charm, before pointing to you in the box and saying: 'I dunno, the defendant looks pretty innocent to me. What do you think?' I doubt it. So make sure you're a learned advocate for the work that you are representing. Show the client that you're

steeped in your subject. Then use your learning to counter any criticism and allay any doubts that might linger in your client's mind.

Believe me, there are few more persuasive words than: 'It has been proven that …'; 'This reminds me of such-and-such a successful viral'; 'We know this works because …'; 'As so-and-so pointed out in his blog/book …'; 'Research has shown us that …'.

Yes, judging creative work *is* all a matter of opinion. But if you can convince your client that your opinion is much better informed than theirs, and if you use that knowledge to back up your argument, then you will have a much better chance of winning them over.

> Show the client that you're steeped in your subject. Then use your learning to counter any criticism and allay any doubts that might linger in your client's mind.

But that's just the first bit of knowledge you need to master. What about the business context?

2 Knowledge of the client's and their competitors' business

If, as we've seen, the client hops from sector to sector then, for the 18 months or so that they're with you, you have got to be their corporate memory. I recommend that, if appropriate, you write a 'brand book' that explains the client's brand idea and the brand values. You should also be able to explain how the competition position themselves and back this up with an archive of their major campaigns. Likewise, you should have all the creative work you've done on the account, plus a brand health record that records results and tells the marketing director what has worked, what hasn't and why.

You can really turn this to your advantage when you're selling work. If the client says they don't like the idea of using animation in the new commercial, you might be able to reassure them that three years ago the brand ran a hugely successful spot with a very similar approach.

Or if they think the work is too aggressive, you may be able to suggest that the competition is currently running a highly effective campaign that is twice as combative.

It could be that the client is uncomfortable with the style of photography. In which case you may be able to point out that this is totally in keeping with the brand's positioning and values.

Again, it is all about winning the client's confidence, trust and respect. If you don't have those then the client will always overrule you. But if you can impress them with your knowledge then, even when the work you're presenting makes them slightly nervous, they will defer to you and accept your recommendations.

> It is all about winning the client's confidence, trust and respect. If you don't have those, then the client will always overrule you.

3 Knowledge of what you're going to say

So far I have covered the general knowledge that will help you to sell your work to clients. Now let's look at the specifics of the sales process.

Once I saw one of our best account directors heading down the corridor with an art bag. 'Where you off to?' I enquired. 'To show the work to the client' replied the account director shaking the art bag. 'That's very nice of you' said I. 'But when are you going off to *sell* it?'

My point then and now is this: the emphasis should always be upon selling. And it takes a lot of concentration and planning.

I was often surprised by colleagues who would sit chatting away in the back of the taxi, when heading off to a big presentation. Perhaps they were better prepared than me, but I was always using the time to rehearse my argument and take yet another look at the work. I'd suggest you focus all your attention on the task in hand, too.

It certainly helps if you get together beforehand to plan your presentation. Knowing what you're going to say is a big advantage that most people fail to grasp because they can't be bothered working it out beforehand. They open their mouths to speak in the hope that what comes out makes a modicum of sense. It usually doesn't.

Very few people can actually think and talk at the same time, so I'd recommend writing down what you're going to say long before you have to say it.

Talk to yourself in the shower, on the bus and as you walk into work

Look at your argument on paper. See if it is clear and tracks properly. Knowing how it sounds is also very useful. So make sure that the sales meeting is not the first time you actually hear your sales pitch. Try to memorise it by practising in the shower on the morning of the presentation. On the train into work. While you're walking from the station to the agency. And say it out loud. (Don't worry, people will think you're talking on your hands-free.) This will help you with such rhythmic details as when to speed up, slow down, pause and where to place your emphases.

You'll look more sincere if you appear to be extemporising. You'll also be more impressive. And remember what I said about clients buying things from people who impress them.

If the sales pitch is a team effort then make sure you've divided the presentation between you and rehearsed it together. Invite someone along to act as your

audience. Make sure they are smart, senior and fearless enough to tell you when you're screwing up. And give them a watch so that they can keep you running to time. Before you begin, you should have a clear idea of how long the meeting is going to last. Make sure you end your presentation with enough time for questions.

Whether you're going to the meeting on your own or as part of a team, there is one person who you need to involve in all your planning. This person won't actually be available for rehearsals. They don't even know they have a part to play. But they are the star of the show. I am, of course, talking about the client.

4 Knowledge of the brief

At the end of Chapter 4 I said getting the client to sign off the brief is probably 'one of the most important parts of the process, yet it is also the one that's so often overlooked … It is also a fundamental part of the selling process.' Here's why.

If you involve the client in writing the brief then you've started selling even before the work begins.

And I mean *involve*. Some clients sign the brief off without looking at it, almost as if they were OKing a requisition order for a consignment of ball-bearings. Their agencies encourage this behaviour by emailing the brief over with little or no explanation of its objective or content. I don't know whether the account people who do this are idle or ignorant. Bit of both, I suppose.

You, I assume, are neither. So you should be talking to the client about all the key issues: the prospect, the problem experienced by the prospect, the solution you'll be selling them and, of course, the proposition that encapsulates all this. They should be familiar with all these elements. Indeed, they should feel as if this is their thinking as much as it is yours.

While you are preparing your sales pitch, have the creative brief in front of you. Keep referring to it and take note of points and details that you know will be useful later.

Then, when the presentation starts, don't just read the brief out – that's the lazy thing to do. Use it to involve the client in your preamble. Make reference to the thinking that they shared when you were writing the brief or comments they've made at other meetings. Use the client's own words. Mention their observations on the target audience; the discussions you had about problem/solution; the shared effort in finding the right proposition; and the client's research that formed the basis of the support points. Position the whole process as a collaborative exercise.

Make sure they agree with everything – especially the proposition. Then get ready to reveal the idea that dramatises or demonstrates that proposition. But do not rush it. Indeed, take the time to exploit the biggest advantage of the lot:

5 Knowledge of the work you are selling

Too many presentations fail because the agency throws away their biggest advantage: they know what the work looks like and the client does not. You should use this knowledge to get the client buying the work in the minutes *before* they actually see it.

If, for example, the client is selling computers and the work features shots of people instead of their beloved product, point out that their own research has shown that this high-tech brand's big problem is its impersonal aspect. Remind them of their own views about the need to humanise the brand. That way, when you reveal the visuals featuring the people, they'll understand the reason why they are there.

Or, if the work has long copy, refer to the client's own insight into how the target audience hungers for information in this category and how they have often said that they want their brand to become that voice of authority.

Or, if you can see that the creative features a large pack-shot, feed back to the client their own view that the customer needs to become familiar with pack design in order to recognise it on the supermarket shelf.

Raise these kind of issues and get the client nodding along with you so that when they eventually see the work it will seem like the only logical way forward.

Take the work apart, bit by bit

Once you've finished the pre-selling, show the work. After a second or two, take the client through every key element. In the following example, I've chosen a press ad, but the same detailed deconstruction applies to everything from a podcast to a radio spot.

Start with the headline – explain why it says what it says. Then the visual – why it looks the way it does. The choice of elements within that visual. The way the work is composed and how all the elements work together to dramatise or demonstrate the proposition. Remind the client of the importance of being abruptive but also the need for relevance.

Read out the first two paragraphs of copy so the client understands how you get from the key elements into the selling zone. Read out all the cross-heads, if there are any, so that the client understands how the sales argument develops. One of the biggest problems you might have in writing the brief is getting the client to focus on a single-minded proposition. They'll want everything in there. So, when you read out the cross-heads, you'll be showing them

> 'Sales' and 'selling' are the watchwords throughout your pitch. That is the client's primary concern and they will reject the work if they feel you don't share their interest.

that you've covered all the selling bases. Finally, read out the call to action. Explain how it will appear and how those leads might then be turned into sales.

Convince the client you're as business-like as they are

As you can see, 'sales' and 'selling' are the watchwords throughout your pitch. That is the client's primary concern and they will reject the work if they feel you don't share their interest. This is particularly important if your agency has developed a reputation for good creative work. Some clients might suspect your motives and assume you've no real interest in business. Disavow them of this thought at every opportunity – especially while you're selling to them.

This applies especially to creative directors and creative teams. Clients will be expecting you to be a bunch of silk-hatted dilettantes. Show yourself to be as hard-nosed as they are. Talk to them about tracking results and let them know that, in your view, work can only be described as 'good' if it has worked.

Taking a creative team to presentations is usually a bright idea. However, if you can't bring them along with you, make sure you know why they've done what they've done. Attend the work-in-progress meeting with a purpose. Ask questions, listen to answers. Keep thinking about the work after the meeting is over. If you've any doubts, go and see the creative team. Perhaps most importantly, study the alternative routes and remember why they were rejected. On occasions a client might suggest doing it another way. If so, tell them it's a good thought but then explain how the team has already explored that option and why it hasn't been pursued.

Know your audience

Try to get a list of who you're presenting to before the meeting begins. There's a good chance that different people have different roles and therefore different objectives for the work. Be aware of these and tailor your presentation so it has something for everyone.

Also, try to make sure that the person who will ultimately sign off the work is present.

This is crucial. Yes, it's fine getting the nod from the junior and middle-weights, but ultimately you need to be sitting opposite the boss if you're going to get a sale. If that simply isn't possible, then do one of two things. Emphasise the fact that you'll be willing to return and present a second time when the boss is available. If that's not possible, give the other clients a written creative rationale to help them sell it upwards.

Whether the boss is present or not, make sure you make eye contact with everyone. Do not single out the decision-maker and focus solely upon them. It's rude and antagonises those you'll have to work with on a daily basis. A colleague of mine used to do this, while ignoring the client's second-in-command. When the boss moved on, the second-in-command took over and fired us within four months.

So address everyone and watch their reactions as the presentation progresses. Once you've taken the clients through the work, shut up. Leave them enough time to assess the work. Then listen carefully to what they say.

> Whether the boss is present or not, make sure you make eye contact with everyone. Do not single out the decision-maker and focus solely upon them.

Do not assume an adversarial stance. Remember James Webb Young's fifth stage in the creative process: 'Shape and develop the idea for practical usefulness.' The client may well have some smart suggestions to make, so greet their ideas with enthusiasm.

Such suggestions often indicate that the client has bought the idea. If so, move them swiftly on. Keep the momentum going. Start talking about the copy, the design and interaction, the photography, the media. Get them to imagine the work in the papers, on screen or in the mail and how the prospect will react to it all.

Listen carefully to what's being said … and even more carefully to what's not

If the client isn't convinced, make sure they explain exactly what is troubling them. As Jon Steel says in his excellent book, *Perfect Pitch*: 'The best communicators, the best persuaders, are the best at what they do because invariably they are good listeners.' So resist leaping in to defend the work until you are certain about their objection. Don't just listen to their words, try to detect the emotion that underpins them. What they're saying may sound quite supportive but the way they say it might betray their real feelings. You must be attuned to this and should subtly pursue the questioning until you get to the nitty-gritty.

Of course, if you've prepared properly then you may have anticipated these problems. In fact, before the sales pitch you should have drawn up a list of the eight most difficult questions you're likely to encounter and you should have worked out the answers and who is going to deliver them.

If the question's a stinker and you're all stumped then it's best to admit humbly 'We don't know' and promise to get back to them with the answer as soon as possible. They'll appreciate being spared the bumbling bullshit. Indeed, they'll probably like your candour and think better of you.

As Jon Steel explains, to be a good salesman you must first be a good listener.

Should you still sense that one of the clients is far from convinced, then do not avoid this person by engaging only with those whose thumbs seem to be pointing upwards. If you leave the room without addressing the sceptic's concerns then, in your absence, they'll almost certainly poison the minds of those who you thought were happy. So focus your attention upon this person. Try to understand their problems and above all let them feel they are being listened to.

One master negotiator was a man called Meyer Lansky, who was, in turn, the financial brain behind Charles Lucania, the most successful Italian-American businessman of the twentieth century.

As this gentleman used to say, 'In negotiations, always leave something for the other guy.'

The secret of Lansky's negotiating skills was simple – 'always leave something for the other guy'. Follow his advice because sometimes this is all it takes to get a sales pitch back on track. Be careful, however, that you only concede points on detail about copy, design or layout. Make sure that the creative idea is left intact.

Your answer, as ever, lies in the brief

Unfortunately, you might find that it is, in fact, the idea that the client is rejecting.

If so, then this is where a tight brief – which has been signed off by the client – is invaluable. Indeed without one you'll be lost in a bout of guesswork and recrimination.

However, when you're armed with a tight brief you can take the client back to the proposition and see if they still agree with it. If they don't, then put the creative back in the art bag and spend the rest of the meeting trying to work out what the new proposition should be. Make sure, however, that the clasp on the art bag is snapped shut because you must not be tempted to get the original work out to see if it will fit the new brief.

If, alternatively, the client still believes the proposition is right then discuss where they think the creative is failing. Remind them that its sole purpose is to dramatise or demonstrate the proposition. Show how it is both abruptive and relevant and argue the case as strongly as you can, using all your knowledge of the historical and business context. When appropriate, you should also play back to them their own concerns, research and advice. If you win them over, thank them and reassure them that this is the strongest selling route they could take.

If you lose, get the hell out of there. Never hang around correcting what is wrong. Not even if you have the creative team with you. Not only does it make it look like you can do creative in a matter of minutes, but it also never works. By the time you're back in the agency, you realise you've agreed to run something you'll all soon regret.

Finally, if it is a sale, remember there is one thing you should do the instant you get back to the agency. Go and see the creative director and the team and let them know how you got on.

If, however, it is a start-again, I'd be inclined to ring the creative director as soon as you leave the meeting. Bad news rarely gets better with waiting. Moreover, it is part of the creative director's job to break that news, explain it to the team and get them motivated again.

Indeed, I've always defined the creative director's job as 'the management of disappointment' and described the ideal CD as a 'charismatic pessimist'. In the final chapter let's take a closer look at how to be a creative director. And find out why it's a title many people covet but a job too few want to do.

How to get the best from a creative department

I closed the last chapter by defining a creative director's job as 'the management of disappointment'. Done properly, it's actually tougher than that. Here's some advice on how to go about it.

On one or two occasions I've given this advice to gatherings of creative directors. Frankly some have been appalled at the impositions I'd be making on their time. But, as I used to remind them, 'That's why they call it "work"'.

Having said that, this is just my version of the job description. Many creative directors who are much better than me will have their own. As will those whose circumstances are different. For much of the time I was, after all, running a smallish department (eight teams). And I had my own agency, so I could do pretty much as I pleased. But they were the most awarded eight teams in our industry and the agency was highly regarded. So make of this what you will.

What's your creative philosophy?

Let's start with creative philosophy. What should it be?

Well, how about this: 'I will never let any crap out of the door.' What's that you say? Not very inspiring? I suppose not. It could also be construed as a little unambitious. But actually it goes to the heart of a creative director's job. For he or she is there to make sure that every assignment is given the same care and attention.

See what I mean about it being a tough job? Of course, you could emulate those who look for the showcase briefs and each year concentrate on doing a handful of ideas that score 9 out of 10 on the 'crap' (2/3) to 'Cannes Lions winner' (9/10) scale. But you'll never get a lasting reputation for good work by cherry-picking assignments in this way.

You'll be much better off turning all the 2s and 3s out of 10 into 4s and 5s. By raising the bar in this way all the 7s become 9s, and every account turns into an account you can be proud of.

Like I said, it's tough, and it demands a refusal to compromise … to let this one through … to turn a blind eye … to fast-track this one out of the door … to say 'OK, that'll do'. It also means getting the entire agency thinking as you do.

Lead the agency not just the department

You've got to have an impact beyond your department. In fact, you should act as a boss of the business. Now I know that

'I will never let
any crap out of
the door.'

nowadays a lot of top creatives like to call themselves 'creative partner' and reckon they are the equal of their 'managing partner'. But most, I'd argue, play the minor role in what is a morganatic relationship.

When it comes to the big decisions on new business, handling existing clients, senior hirings, pay rises, etc., they defer to the managing director and often aren't even alerted, never mind consulted, when the lorry-load of fresh compromises pulls up outside the agency each day.

If you're a creative director and you don't see yourself this way then take this simple test: do you know how much your managing director and CEO earn? If not, why not? And why are you allowing yourself to be marginalised?

As I said above, I had the advantage of running my own agency. And I was doubly fortunate because my two managing partners, Tim Patten and Martin Troughton, never once deviated from their commitment to better creative or the processes that made it possible.

I wish you the same luck. I would also warn you not to become so enamoured of life at the managerial big table that it distracts you from your day job. Indeed, to have a lasting impact on the agency at large you've got to make sure you're always doing the departmental job properly.

Become the best paid traffic manager in the business

A good creative director knows what each team is working on and where they are in the creative process.

If that sounds like the role of the traffic manager, well, that's precisely what I was when I was doing the job. The best paid traffic manager in the business.

I suggest you do the same and start by getting all the account teams together every Friday morning for a 'control meeting'. Here's how it should work: you go round the room asking the account director of each group what creative briefs are coming in over the next four weeks. Then you take their orders.

The first account director might say that in week 2 they'll have a brief for an SMS, two new banner ads and a page takeover. In week 3, they'll need to brief a new press campaign and week 4 they'll want to brief in amends to a set of fulfilment brochures. Jot that down and then go to the next account director. In week 1, they'll have a brief for a new radio spot. In week 2 they'll need one or maybe two teams for an integrated on and offline campaign. Make a note of that and move on. The next account director simply confirms the web redesign brief they've been expecting and that it is, as noted at last week's meeting,

> A good creative director knows what each team is working on and where they are in the creative process.

arriving this week (i.e. week 1). And so it goes until you've taken orders from each account group.

In a mid-size agency this should take about 30 minutes.

Now there'll be those who'll complain about waiting around while other people discuss their work. And some business directors might say that they've got more pressing things to do than see what's happening on the creative front. If so, then ask them what could be more important than the work their clients are paying the agency to do? Then insist they attend – and don't start the meeting until they turn up.

Similarly, some account directors might say the whole thing is a waste of time (and money in billable hours). Just tell them they're guilty of one of the biggest sins committed in client service: silo thinking. They go about their business oblivious to the existence of their colleagues and ignorant of the problems and solutions they could share. This meeting is their opportunity to begin this collegiate approach. It's also a valuable weekly 'town meeting' at which other issues can be discussed, questions asked and news transmitted.

Once the issues, questions and news are dealt with, the creative director is armed with a list of every new brief that's coming into the creative department over the next month. Now all they have to do is find someone to do them.

In most agencies this allocation is, for some reason, done by the traffic manager. Why? What do they know about the capabilities of each creative team? How do they know who is suited to an IT brief and who might do better on retail work? And how can they tell when a team needs a 'softer' brief to work on after weeks of struggling on a particularly tough assignment? Moreover, how do they know how long a team might need on a particular job?

Only the creative director can make such decisions. Most importantly, if the traffic manager does the allocation then the creative director has already lost control of the work. For, if the creative director abdicates responsibility at this early stage, they'll never develop the sense of knowing exactly where each job is at any given time.

Make sure everyone knows exactly what they're doing

Once the creative director has allocated all incoming briefs to the various teams for the next four weeks, they should write it down on a control sheet and pin it up all over the agency.

This tells the creative teams exactly what they'll be working on and when their deadlines are. It also alerts account people as to when their briefs need to be written and signed off. Just as importantly, the control sheet tells the account people which teams are taken – and in a well-run department that should mean all of them.

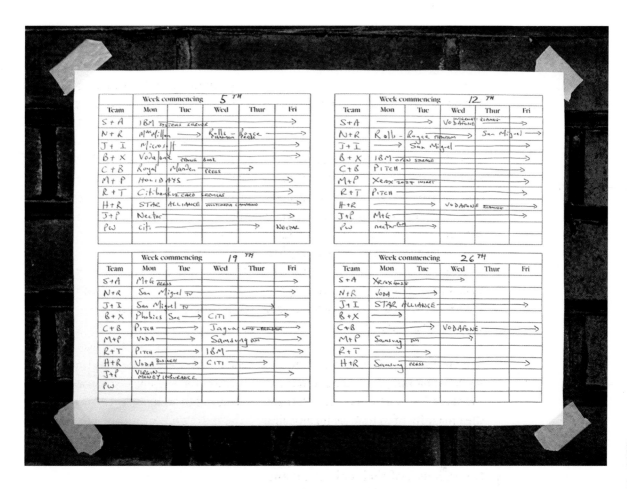

So if they suddenly get a rush job they know they cannot elbow their other account-handling colleagues aside and 'slip' the emergency brief into the creative department.

If a rush job *is* necessary, then the account person needs to tell the 'best paid traffic manager' in town. This is vital. No job should ever go into the creative department without the creative director's knowledge and, indeed, permission.

Which, after traffic manager, brings us to the next big role played by the creative director: quality controller of the creative brief.

Get the briefs and the timings right

Quite simply, no brief can make it to the creative floor without the creative director's signature. Which means the creative director is there to demand a rethink on dual propositions, non-existent budgets, fact-free support points and briefs that focus on the client's problem and not the prospect's.

I always used to do the control sheet by hand. I thought it brought a touch of humanity to the process. Others said it was also a courageous account person who dared amend my version.

The creative director is also there to stop impossible timing plans being imposed upon the team. A major part of any manager's job lies in being clear about what they want their people to do and then making sure they have the time to do it.

If all that is needed is a change to existing creative, then the creative director needs to look at the amends brief and work out how long it'll take to complete those amends. If, however, the brief is for a new concept, then the creative director should be allowing a minimum of five days from the team taking the brief to the final choice of the work that will be presented to the client.

I know that some of you might think this sounds like a long time, and that your clients may want it sooner. If so, remember that the team need time for the first four stages of James Webb Young's process (if you want a reminder, please take a look at page 7). And also bear in mind that they'll be working simultaneously on the previous weeks' ideas, i.e. on Young's final stage 5: 'Shaping and developing those ideas for practical usefulness.' Which means, when you think about it, five days is no time at all if you want a quality product. If, however, having *thought* about it your client still complains then ask them this rhetorical question: 'Why is it that there's never time to do it right but there's always time to do it again?'

> Why is it that there's never time to do it right but there's always time to do it again?

How to run a WIP

After that, it's the creative director's job to make sure the ideas flow as the work moves smoothly through the department. Which means attending every work-in-progress meeting. A WIP is a meeting with the team roughly halfway through the creative process. It is crucial for a couple of reasons. First, it allows the creative director to remain aware of the team's progress and whether they're going to hit their deadlines. It also allows the creative director an opportunity to sort the good thinking from the bad and steer the team towards the big creative idea.

If, as I say, the team will be using you as a sounding board, they should have lots of ideas to show you. Tell them not to bother working them up on the Mac or having them drawn beautifully. Their time is better spent coming up with more and more ideas. These should then be written up or roughly sketched out on an A3 layout pad and stuck on the wall.

When you look at these initial ideas, you have to make sure the team is working to the proposition and not just an aspect of the brief that looks like it could be fruitful or fun to work on. I always used to like my teams to have the proposition pinned above their desks. It helped them remain focused. In similar vein, you need to decide if the work is designed to sell the product.

Creative teams have been known to do work that looks wonderful on their wall and which wins the praise of passing colleagues. Whether the work will actually sell anything is by the by.

Make sure you quickly kill the self-indulgent and off-brief work and take down the ideas you've seen before. Then look at what remains and see if the ideas are abruptive enough to get noticed and relevant enough to convince the prospect that this product might be worth buying.

> Always try to be constructive. There is no value in pointing out the problems unless you're able to propose some kind of solution.

See the work through the eyes of the prospect

Think of the environment in which the work will be seen and anticipate the prospect's level of involvement at the time the message is delivered. Ask yourself:

- Will the prospect notice it?
- Will they be interested enough to engage with it?

Find ways in which the ideas might be made more impactful and specific to the product or the prospect (or both). Once you've done that, give the team a steer by suggesting other ways in which they can dramatise or demonstrate the proposition.

Always try to be constructive. There is no value in pointing out the problems un-less you're able to propose some kind of solution. And be sensitive, too. You've probably just picked apart days of hard graft, and the junior and less strong teams will need their spirits lifting (re-member what I said about this job being the management of disappointment?).

The better teams will bounce back and see your critique for what it is – a great opportunity to do something better. This resilience is, indeed, the hallmark of the very best creatives. As the handbook that Crispin Porter + Bogusky give to their employees says: 'It takes a special person to succeed here, one who has passion, confidence and the work ethic to believe in their ability to come up with more great ideas if and when their original great idea dies.'

Know when your people are down 'love–40' and get them back to 'deuce'

Unfortunately we can't all work with such creative Spartans and occasionally, when time and inspiration are tight, it's necessary for creative directors to sit down and crack the brief themselves.

This ability to sense when your people are down 'love–40' and the energy and expertise to get them back to 'deuce' is, I think, the measure of good management on agency and client side alike.

Unfortunately a lot of managers nowadays rarely venture out to Court 17 to see how their people are doing. They're too busy in the executive box at Centre Court, i.e. spending all their time managing the expectations and experience of the people above them so they, in turn, look good to the bosses. Instead of giving guidance to the people below them, they encourage their staff to follow suit and play politics and 'raise their own profiles'. This leads to the survival of the devious and the pursuit not of quality but ever-more elaborate job titles. Given such corrupt management, is it any wonder there's the general dissatisfaction in the workplace to which I alluded in Chapter 2?

Of course, yours will be a happier workplace – and to keep it that way you'll sometimes have to step in and produce a 7-out-of-10 idea when the team is struggling with 2s and 3s. On the very rare occasion when neither the creative director nor the team can crack the brief, it is the creative director's job to inform the account director that more time is needed. If the account team resist, they just need to be reminded that the client will soon forget that you were three days late but they'll never forgive bad work that bombed.

> Many senior managers are more comfortable getting into groups to write briefs and devise strategies because, frankly, it's easier than sitting down and doing it on their own.

Avoid management by committee

Which brings me to the creative director's most obvious role: ensuring that the best work is always presented. This means having the final say on which work is developed after the initial WIP and also the last word on which work gets sold to the client.

Some people may not like this. Indeed, I know we live in an open-sourced age where there's wisdom in crowds and 'no one is smarter than everyone'. I also suspect that many senior managers are more comfortable getting into groups to write briefs and devise strategies because, frankly, it's easier than sitting down and doing it on their own. Getting into a huddle to come up with the best creative work is also fashionable. Indeed, many agencies now like to invite the client to these brainstorming meetings.

I can't see the sense in this. If you subscribe to James Webb Young's technique for producing ideas then you'll know the big ones pop out of the subconscious when you least expect them. They're certainly not waiting around to make a guest appearance during the brainstorming session that the head of planning's PA has set up 'twixt 10.00 and 11.00 am in Conference Room 3.

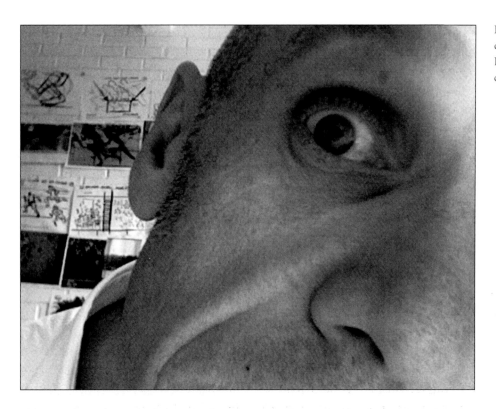

Everybody's favourite creative genius, Tony Kaye, is also against creativity by committee.

No, I'm afraid I'm with David Ogilvy and his views on the group decision: 'Search the parks in all your cities, you'll find no statues of committees.' If that seems like a voice from another age, here's everybody's favourite creative genius, Tony Kaye: 'Collaboration only works when it is siphoned by a singular vision.' Or, if you're still not convinced, here's Mark Fiddes, executive creative director at Draftfcb, London, writing in *Campaign* about the damaging effect of brainstorming on the creative output of UK agencies: 'The UK is the tectonic epicentre of brainstorming. While they can make clients feel like Leonardo da Vinci for an afternoon, the creative workshop often serves only to work over a creative idea until it is pulped.

Too often, promising thinking is hijacked by folk with little intuition for what engages customers.'

If anyone still questions this then they should be shown the creative director's business card and reminded of the job title. This, after all, is supposed to be the creative director's area of expertise.

You should be able to look at all the ideas at the final review and choose the one you feel best dramatises or demonstrates the proposition. Not only that, you should ensure that that idea is also the most suitable for the target audience and best reinforces the brand idea (if there is one).

On more than one occasion I made the mistake of choosing a very abruptive and relevant idea but failed to anticipate that the target audience would not tolerate the tone of voice in which it was delivered. So make sure you assess the work against all three criteria and then engage your peers in an open discussion about the relative merits of each piece and explain your choice. Again, this shouldn't become a free-for-all. As Alan Bennett says in his play *Forty Years On*: 'I'm all in favour of free expression, provided it is kept rigidly under control.'

You're running a creative department not a pizza parlour

During your internal discussions there's one criterion that should never be considered: which idea will the client buy. Yes I know the client is paying the bills. But the client is also paying the agency for their years of experience and expertise. So earn your fees and present the one idea that fits the criteria mentioned above. You'll note I said, 'the one idea'. This used to be common practice in the best agencies, but nowadays few have the courage to take one agency recommendation to the client.

They prefer to show them three or more ideas until the client sees one they like. As I said in the previous chapter, the client's expectations will probably have been set by what has already been done in the category. In most cases even the most reasonable client will, if given the choice, err on the side of caution. They'll tell you that they'd like to take the work away and think about it, then two days later they'll call you to say 'We really like the more unconventional route and, yes, we'll run it in the autumn, but for now we'll be going with our first choice.' Of course, come autumn the budget will have been reallocated, the marketing director will have left and the work will remain forever consigned to the team's bottom drawer.

So if you want the best work to run, then go and sell it – and it alone.

If the client still insists on seeing more executions then take rough scamps of the best three other ideas and use them to explain why the agency recommendation is by far the strongest. Be careful though. You're still in danger of the client choosing the weaker route. Worse still, they might even take one element from the agency recommendation and something from the other three, to create the 'pizza topping' of their choice – which no one, least of all the prospect, will like.

Don't rob Production Peter to pay Creative Paul

Don't forget that once you've sold the work, you have to ensure it can actually be produced.

This means working closely throughout the process with the people from production. In digital especially they have to be involved from day one, otherwise you run the risk of coming up with an idea that cannot be executed without an elastic timeline and a budget that would make George Lucas's eyes water.

I was lucky to have two heads of production, Vidhu Kapur and Donna Brown, who, in eight years, never once sucked their teeth, shook their heads and said, 'Oooh no, it can't be done'. Many of the things we gave them had never been executed before. But they exhausted every possible option to get them out on budget, on time and to the highest specification. In return, I tried to protect their interests. I suggest you do the same with your production people.

Too often the extra time that's bought to make sure the creative is correct comes at their expense. Production Peter, so to speak, is robbed to pay Creative Paul. It's a false economy. So when

> When WIPs are called, make sure there is a production person present to assess whether the big idea can be done to schedule and with the money that's available.

timing plans are devised, be sure to check with production that there are enough hours in there for them to do their job properly. And when WIPs are called, make sure there is a production person present to assess whether the big idea in gestation can actually be done to schedule and with the money that's available.

And that is that on the day-to-day running of the creative department. I reckon that if the creative director does all this then, after 12 months, their clients and their colleagues will have a lot of work they can be proud of.

Then it's time to get your frocks out

The question then is, should the agency enter the work into awards? Well, there are some agencies who pooh-pooh them, but that's usually because they know they have no chance of winning. I, however, think they're a great idea. Especially those in direct marketing that are linked to sales performance.

Such a commitment, however, adds yet another job title to the long list held by the creative director: that of awards coordinator.

The task begins with picking the right awards to enter. At HTW we limited ourselves to just three or four awards shows that we aimed to dominate.

Why so choosy? Well, entering awards is expensive. And done properly it is hard work. It involves selecting the right pieces, choosing the right categories and preparing the entries for presentation. This can't be delegated. Because they'll probably have sat on many awards juries, only the creative director will know what the judges are looking for and which work is good enough to catch their eye.

Moreover, past experience will mean the CD knows better than anyone how to write the submissions, if a few well-chosen words of explanation are needed.

You should give these jobs your full attention because, among other things, winning awards can also win you new business.

Awards are good during new business meetings, for you can use comparison tables like this to put your rivals' claims to creative pre-eminence in perspective.

During the pitching process you'll no doubt hear about your rival agencies' claims to creative pre-eminence. So, when you take your prospective client on the tour of your agency, make sure you swing by the Trophy Room. It will quickly put your competitors' claims into perspective.

Share the glory with everyone

At HTW we also took awards seriously because we knew the value of a good night out. Awards are a wonderful reward for the very hard work that goes into creating effective work. Moreover, in my experience, clients love the glamour and glory more than agency people do. And why shouldn't they? Never forget that without their wisdom, money and yes, in many cases, courage, you wouldn't be there. So get them up on stage.

Although your receptionists, HR, finance people, PAs and other support staff don't play a direct role in the creative process,

Precision Marketing Creative League Table May 2005

Agency	Response	Echo	IDM	DMA	Campaign	Cannes	Total	May-05	Oct-04	Apr-04	Oct-03
Harrison Troughton Wunderman	0	0	8	90	56	29	183	1	1	1	1
Tequila (all offices, inc. TBWA/GGT)	24	11	6	24	12	12	89	2	-	-	-
Craik Jones Watson Mitchell Voelkel	21	1	0	50	10	5	87	3	2	3	3
Publicis Dialog	29	0	0	25	16	12	82	4	3	8	10
Saatchi & Saatchi	0	0	2	30	26	19	77	5	4	2	2
WWAV Rapp Collins (all offices)	21	7	8	15	0	0	51	6	9	6	5
Tullo Marshall Warren	5	0	0	27	12	4	48	7	12=	20=	25=
Proximity London	13	0	0	18	12	4	47	8	8	10	9
Archibald Ingall Stretton	28	0	0	8	9	0	45	9	5	4	4
Partners Andrews Aldridge	7	0	0	21	16	0	44	10	6	5	6
ARC (inc Leonardo)	16	0	0	10	14	2	42	11	7	7	7
20:20 London	23	0	0	0	10	4	37	12	15	22	22
Euro RSCG	8	0	0	8	12	7	35	13	11	23	21
EHS Brann (all offices)	5	0	2	14	10	3	34	14	16	14	12
Draft London (inc Lowe Love & Plus)	12	6	0	8	0	5	31	15	14	11	11
OgilvyOne	4	3	0	12	8	3	30	16	17	13	15
Story	0	5	0	22	0	0	27	17	18	15=	-
Different	0	0	0		16	0	20	18	19	17	17=
Rapier											

they are just as integral to the agency culture and play their part in generating an environment in which good ideas thrive. So try to squeeze them on stage if you can.

Otherwise, make sure you crack open a few bottles in the agency the following day. Such shindigs aren't just fun, they are vital to the perpetuation of the culture you are trying to create. All cultures need to be seen to be succeeding, otherwise individuals begin to question their mores and values, and start to deviate from the rituals. Before you know it, horror of horrors, people will start slipping work into the creative department without a brief and be expecting to see something by end of play.

So celebrate your successes. And you'll find this will encourage your people to achieve even greater things. You'll also end up with a very pleasant hangover – after some fabulous nights out.

I've had more than my fair share of both. And I hope that the preceding pages help you to achieve much the same. But as the hangover clears on the morning after, there are two things you can do to make sure that the agency avoids failure in the future and that you aren't destroyed by success.

First, start worrying that you'll never repeat last night's performance and, to banish complacency, convey that restless insecurity to the rest of the agency.

Then thank God for your good fortune, try to be humble in His sight and remember these words from the Alexandrian Greek poet Constantine Cavafy: 'Ancient houses are not eternal/ Of course, many people will have much to say/ We shall listen. But we will not be deceived/ by words such as Indispensable, Unique and Great/Someone else indispensable and unique and great/can always be found at a moment's notice.'

Conclusion
I hope I haven't wasted your time

You're very lucky. If I'd written this five years ago, you'd have had to plough through a much bigger book. But the longer I worked and the better I got at my job, the simpler everything became: two big ideas … problem/solution … relevant abruption … and sufficient time to do it all properly. Is there really much more to it? Isn't it just 'a simple game made complicated by fools'?

I began by appropriating that quote from football legend, Bill Shankly. I conclude with one from the finest cricketer of all time, Don Bradman. A young Australian, new to the national side, was too in awe of 'The Don' to ask him for advice about his technique, so he persuaded another team member to approach the great man. The response? 'Tell your mate that if he keeps the ball on the ground then he won't get out.'

Isn't it the same with what we do: get the basics right and you won't go wrong? Well, not according to the fashionable thinking in our industry.

Is it 'time to throw out all the old rules and beliefs'?

Judging by the trade press and the industry grapevine it would appear things are changing at such a frantic rate that it's well-nigh impossible to write a book about creativity that acknowledges any debt to the past. Indeed, most might say you've been wasting your time by reading it.

For example, when invited to speak at the International Congress of Brand Trends in Spain, I was honoured to share the stage with creative stars from that country and Latin America. But I was also worried I was going to be a huge disappointment when I read the blurb: 'We can say that the rules of the game have changed. What worked years ago is no longer effective. We have to change our way of thinking.'

That was in February 2009. Some 12 months earlier I'd noticed the same fixation with change in *Advertising Age*'s 'Trends to Watch'. Here is Bob Liodice, president and CEO of the American Association of National Advertisers: 'A new kind of marketing professional is emerging – individuals with a holistic view of the world and extraordinary observational powers. These "renaissance" marketers will be part humanist, part psychologist, part anthropologist and part technologist.'

Back in the UK, the chair of the Direct Marketing Association's Agency Council, explained: 'When the Wright Brothers first flew it was a consequence of writing new rules. They believed they had to start again and write rules from scratch. To throw out all the old rules and beliefs. DM is in the same position now. It's on the brink of a new era.'

'You're not afraid of change, are you?'

This isn't just bad aviation history. It is also, I believe, a dangerous analysis of how we should face the future. Dangerous, because it is typical of the conventional wisdom that dismisses all that's been learned on both agency and client side. And dangerous also because it delivers that future into the hands of those whose 'extraordinary observational powers' allow them to detect a very convenient bandwagon rolling by.

Convenient? Well, yes. Because it's easier to talk the transitional talk than it is to sit down at your desk and do the things that I've described in the previous eight chapters: steeping yourself in your business, studying your customer, learning your trade, applying its principles, adapting them to new circumstances and passing your knowledge on to your staff. It seems that in the current climate any one who holds fast to such practices is seen as reactionary. Indeed, on agency and client side alike, the most unanswerable denunciation anyone can deliver is to arch an eyebrow and ask in rhetorical fashion: 'You're not afraid of change, are you?'

> It's easier to talk the transitional talk than it is to sit down at your desk and do the things that I've described in the previous eight chapters.

Personally, not as long as that change is built on humanist principles that lead to cultures moving forward and individuals gaining enlightenment through the constant accumulation of knowledge.

Unfortunately I don't see a lot of that going on. Instead of corporate humanism there's a creeping barbarism that damns much of the understanding gained from the past as irrelevant.

Bumped into any charlatans or half-wits today?

Dr Alan Tapp, Professor of Marketing at Bristol Business School, explained to me the damage caused by such superficiality: 'If best practice has little or no value, what does? The answer is the Cult of the New. In a world that lacks substance, fads and fashions take over and marketers are obsessed with change and the next big thing.'

Malcolm McDonald, Emeritus Professor of Marketing at Cranfield University, is equally critical. In his opinion the marketing discipline has lost respect because 'lots of charlatans and half-wits have got into it without qualifications'.

But maybe, just maybe, the past really is no guide to a future when it comes to mastering the skills and performing the roles now expected on both agency and client side.

In Chapter 2 I quoted the hero of Richard Yates's novel *Revolutionary Road*. Here he is again listening to his boss talk about who is going to take the lead in a complex, ever-changing business world:

'Your public relations expert? Your electronics engineer? Your management consultant? Well, now, certainly all of them are going to play important roles in the overall picture; each of them is going to offer very valuable specialised knowledge in their respective fields. But here's the point. No single one of them has the right background or the right qualifications for the job. I've talked to some of the top advertising and promotions men in the business. I've talked to some of the top technical men in the computer field and I've talked to some of the top administration men in the country, and we've all of us pretty much come to this conclusion: it's a completely new kind of job and we're going to have to develop a completely new kind of talent to do it.'

Yates certainly seems to understand the problem of how, in a world of change, to find the homo novus with the necessary vision and skills to lead everyone forward. Except for the fact that Yates was writing in 1961 and set his novel in 1955. Some 53 years, in fact, before Bob Liodice spied his renaissance marketer with 'extraordinary observational powers' skipping over the horizon.

Quite clearly nothing is new here. Everyone who is any good usually, at some point, feels insecure about and, yes, threatened by the future. But throwing the baby, which it's taken nearly a hundred years to nurture, out with the bathwater is absolutely no response to the challenges being faced at the moment.

To finish, let me leave you with something written at roughly the same time as that passage from *Revolutionary Road*:

'It took millions of years for man's instincts to develop. It will take millions more for them to even vary. It is fashionable to talk about "changing man". A communication must be concerned with "unchanging man", with his obsessive drive to survive, to be admired, to succeed, to love, to take care of his own.'

These are the words of Bill Bernbach. Perhaps even the people who are most committed to complicating our simple game will respect his views and follow his advice.

Index

Acknowledgements

If I've enjoyed some success in my career then it's largely down to working *with* colleagues who were industrious and talented and *for* clients who were shrewd and brave enough to buy the work we did.

My good fortune has persisted during this foray into publishing. Having written my manuscript I was lucky enough for it to be read by Sam Jackson at Pearson Education. She's taken a chance on and helped guide this previously unpublished author and I am very grateful to her for doing so. I would also like to thank her colleagues Emma Devlin and Josephine Bryan, who as desk and copy editors, could not have been more fastidious. Suffice to say, I'd hate to be the one to leave the cap off the toothpaste in their bathrooms. The same dedication has been shown by Caroline Jordan who has worked like a Trojan on the research and admin jobs that've brought this book to publication.

Speaking of which, we couldn't have gathered together all the creative work that's featured in the book without the help and generosity of these individuals: Robert Corbishley at Xerox; Alan Flack at IBM; Gavin Hill-Smith at the AA; Anna Caig and Nicki Lidbetter at Anxiety UK (formerly The National Phobics Society); Daniel Ramsey at the British Heart Foundation and Mike Parsons who took the shot for the BHF's campaign; Rebecca Emery at Amnesty International Aotearoa, New Zealand; Chiara Lamma, Ben More, James Kennedy and Giles Morris at Sony UK; Ysabel Vazquez at Mini; Michelle Rowley at Macmillan Cancer Relief; Harry Ward at Help the Aged; Santiago Mazon at Banco Gallego; Emma Knight at Honda; Gonzalo Lanata at Papa John's Peru; Uwe Lussem and Heino Hilbig at Olympus Europa; Ralf Maltzen and Torsten Skoracki at Volkswagen; Deepa B Bose and Louise D Muhlauer at American Express; and Sean O'Donnell at Speight's Beer.

On the agency side, I would like to express my gratitude to Meike Scharnhorst and Amir Kassaei at DDB Berlin; Tanja Braune and Sandra Atwell at Springer and Jacoby Werbeagentur, Hamburg; Dave King at AIM Proximity, New Zealand; Nick Worthington at Colenso BBDO, New Zealand; Karl Fleet, Evaan Miocevich, Lachlan McPherson and Martin Yeoman at Publicis Mojo, New Zealand; Sarah Cooper at AMV BBDO, London; Brendan Tansey at Wunderman, London; Gail McClelland, Kim Papworth and Neil Christie at Wieden + Kennedy, London; Rebecca Leggett at DDB, London; Stephen Sapka, Katie Kempner and Alex Bogusky at Crispin Porter + Bogusky; and Mauricio Paez at Quorum Nazca Saatchi & Saatchi, Peru.

When it came to rummaging for not just ads but also stats on the M&G case study, I should also thank Joanna King of the Insitute of Direct Marketing's Business Performance Awards and Steve Martin of the Account Planning Group's Creative Planning Awards. I am also very grateful to Maxine Delahunty of SOFII which provides a very useful showcase of fundraising innovation and inspiration; Jamie Gunn at comScore and Kathrine Everard at the IPA.

For providing valuable help and advice on content and style I'm indebted to Kevan Ansell, Mark Fiddes, Polly Jones, Simon Sinclair and my cousin Iain Harrison.

And for their guidance and encouragement I would like to thank my expert readers Jon Steel, Paul Ferraiolo, Larissa Vince, Charlie Smith, Pablo Alzugaray, Hugh Burkitt and especially Mark Cridge for being so adroit and alert.

If those individuals have made the book read a lot better then David Eldridge, its designer, and his colleague Kevan Westbury, have made it look splendid. So a big thanks to them, too.

I'd also like to take this opportunity to pay tribute to my late friend Christopher Radcliffe Dearden whose inspiring courage in the face of both MS and bipolar disorder helped put in perspective the relatively minor problems I encountered while trying to run an agency and get some ads out. May God rest his soul.

And finally and most importantly I'd like to acknowledge the love and support of Morag Brennan. Throughout the low points she never let me forget that the whole thing was supposed to be an adventure. And during the high points I always knew that the best thing to come was waiting for me at home.

Publisher's acknowledgements

The publisher would like to thank the following for their kind permission to reproduce their images:

Page 24, © Tim Klein/Stone/Getty Images; Page 36, The History of Advertising Trust; Page 37, American Express; Page 39, Mini UK; Page 40, The Economist; Page 41, Help The Aged; Page 42, Mike Parsons and the British Heart Foundation; Page 46, Peter Funch and Sony UK Ltd; Page 71, The AA; Page 73, Gonzalo Lanata D. and Papa Johns; Page 75, Honda (UK), Weiden and Kennedy and The History of Advertising Trust; Page 77, Amnesty International (NZ); Page 79, Olympus Imaging Europa GmBH; Page 81, with permission of IBM UK Ltd; Page 83, Xerox Ltd; Page 85, Anxiety UK (formerly The National Phobics Society); Page 87, Macmillan Cancer Support; Pages 95-101 © Account Planning Group, www.apg.org.uk and IDM Business Performance Awards; Page 104, Lion Nathan and Speights; Pages 105-106, Volkswagen AG; Page 121, from *Perfect Pitch* by Jon Steel. Copyright © John Wiley & Sons, Inc. 2006. Reproduced with permission of John Wiley & Sons, Inc; Page 122, © Bettmann/CORBIS.

Every effort has been made to trace the copyright holders and we apologise in advance for any unintentional omissions.